BALANCING ACTS

More Than 250 Guiltfree, Creative Ideas to Blend Your Work and Your Life

BARBARA A. GLANZ

D1416912

Dearborn™
Trade Publishing
A **Kaplan Professional** Company

This publication is designed to provide accurate and authoritative information in regard to the subject matter covered. It is sold with the understanding that the publisher is not engaged in rendering legal, accounting, or other professional service. If legal advice or other expert assistance is required, the services of a competent professional should be sought.

Vice President and Publisher: Cynthia A. Zigmund
Senior Managing Editor: Jack Kiburz
Interior and Cover Designs: Scott Rattray, Rattray Design
Typesetting: the dotted i

Every effort has been made to locate the copyright owners of the material used in this book. If an error or omission has been made, please notify the publisher and necessary changes will be made in subsequent printings.

Published by Dearborn Trade Publishing
A Kaplan Professional Company

Printed in the United States of America

03   04   05   06   07   10   9   8   7   6   5   4   3   2   1

Library of Congress Cataloging-in-Publication Data

Glanz, Barbara A.
    Balancing acts : more than 250 guiltfree, creative ideas to blend your work and your life / Barbara A. Glanz.
        p.   cm.
    Includes bibliographical references and index.
    ISBN 0-7931-6520-2 (6x8 paperback)
    1. Work and family.   I. Title.
HD4904.25.G58 2003
650.1—dc21

2003001185

Praise for *Balancing Acts*

"Most people today find it impossible to create 'balance' between their work and family. Barbara Glanz's new book offers hope and help to workers and managers alike. Her caring, enthusiastic spirit will touch your heart and move you to action!"

—Ken Blanchard, Coauthor of *The One Minute Manager*

"Life balance: buzzword or reality? Everyone talks about it, and many try to achieve balance by giving up something in favor of something else. That's exchange, not balance. The answer is blending, finding the right mixture for you. Through experience and examples, Barbara Glanz engages us and illuminates our path. Fresh approach; well worth reading."

—Roger E. Herman, Consulting Futurist, Author of *Lean & Meaningful* and other books, and Chief Executive Officer, The Herman Group, Greensboro, North Carolina

"Barbara Glanz has done us all a favor by identifying the increasing desire for life/work balance and for providing so many good examples of practical ways to accomplish this goal. She makes a nice transition from the sometimes onerous challenge of 'balance' to one of 'blending' the key spheres of our lives. This easy-to-read, accessible tool for individuals and organizations will find eager readers both in the workplace and at home."

—Ann McGee-Cooper, Ed.D., Author of *You Don't Have to Go Home from Work Exhausted!*

"Packed with practical and useful ideas for individuals as well as organizations, *Balancing Acts* provides readers with resources and solutions for every stage of their lives. Specifically, the section on spirit is an important addition to work-life solutions, and one that is often neglected."

— Bonnie Michaels, President, Managing Work & Family, Inc.

"This book delivers exactly what it promises—a huge collection of creative ideas for blending, balancing, easing, and enriching your work and life. For anyone who wants a life, and a valuable addition to any company's work-life library!"

— Susan Seitel, President, Work & Family Connection, Inc.

"It takes a class act to know how to produce a balancing act. Barbara Glanz is that and has done that. She will provide you with 250 gems, absolute jewels, to sparkle and glitter with that connective tissue between the balanced place that you work and the balanced home where you love."

— Bob Danzig, Former President of Hearst Newspapers, Author, and Professional Speaker

"*Balancing Acts* is a beautifully crafted book that will be helpful for individuals, as well as their organizations, with very specific, practical ideas. The powerful simplicity of the ideas presented is reflected in the stories and examples shared throughout the book."

— Kate Larsen, PCC President/Coach, Winning LifeStyles, Inc.

In loving dedication:

- To my own family—my children, Garrett, Gretchen, and Erin, my children-in-love, Ashley and Randy; and my most precious grandchildren, Gavin and Kinsey.
- To all families everywhere who are struggling to find more time together, and
- To our Lord who created families as His messengers here on earth.

TO MY READERS

It is rather ironic that while I have been writing a book on balance, I have been experiencing one of the most *unbalanced* periods of my entire life! Two and a half years ago my precious husband, Charlie, died of cancer, and ever since, I have been trying to decide what to do with the rest of my life. Having married at 21, right out of college, I went from one protected environment to another. I never before have had my own place to live nor have I ever bought or owned a car in my own name. So, after nearly 34 years of marriage, all of a sudden I have been forced to start a new life alone.

It IS a couple's world, and I have found that I no longer feel welcome at places where I once was. My work as a professional speaker and author has given me a deep sense of purpose and mission, but I have found myself working day and night, partly because of the calling I feel but also as an anesthetic to soften the pain.

Several months ago I decided that I must begin to bring some joy into my life again, and because I no longer seemed to fit in the suburbs where our family home had been for the past 33 years, I began to think about where I would like to live. Just after Charlie had his first surgery, we bought a small place on Siesta Key in Sarasota, Florida, which was a dream come true for Charlie. We spent the last three months of his life there in the spring of 2000. Each winter since his death, I have gone to Sarasota for part of the winter, where I have written a new book. Because the ocean has been so healing for me, I decided that perhaps that was where I should think about moving.

This spring a condo right on the ocean in the same association became available, and it seemed as if it were a gift from God, albeit a very expensive one! Everyone on the staff at Horizons West wanted me to buy it. Finally in May, I made the decision to close on the property. However, the whole unit needed to be gutted, so ever since, wonderful folks have been renovating it for me.

For months I was not sure if I could do this all alone, with so many, many decisions to make and such emotional trauma from leaving behind everything familiar—as well as sometimes experiencing devastating lone-liness without my husband. My children all live far away, so they are rarely available to help, and because I travel nearly every week in my work, I have had to back away from relationships that were extremely important to me, so my support system has dwindled considerably. As we all know, there simply is not time for everything!

In June I put my house in Illinois up for sale, another traumatic event, and it became even more traumatic when it took longer than expected to sell. Since June, I have felt as if I were "living in midair!" I did not belong in *either* Illinois or Florida.

When the house finally did sell, I had just six weeks to sort through and pack 27 years of "stuff" all alone, go on six different speaking engagements, including one to Caracas, Venezuela, hire a new full-time assistant in Florida and find office space there, *and* finish this book. In fact, the manuscript was due to the publisher the SAME DAY the movers were coming, so you can imagine my stress level as I have been writing! *Talk about a balancing act!*

The lesson I have been learning again and again is the one reiterated in this book: Only through BLENDING *work and life* can we survive the stress and upheaval most of us face on a daily basis. I will be eternally grateful to many friends who volunteered to help me pack (FRIENDS). Several of them were also professional speakers, so we shared business ideas as we filled boxes (WORK). Others were friends from my church, and we shared spiritual needs and concerns as we sorted and packed (SPIRIT). My family helped out in long-distance ways, with my son helping me to refinance two mortgages and my daughters and son-in-love helping with different aspects of my speaking business (FAMILY).

Walking up and down three flights of stairs MANY times a day provided the exercise I needed, and although I stopped cooking, with Lean Cuisine I enjoyed a somewhat well-rounded diet (HEALTH). And, finally, I loved being able to give so many things away to people and groups that could really use and enjoy them (SERVICE). Even though it was hard to let go of many things that had sentimental value, the joy in sharing with others precluded the pain.

As I write this I am in the final days of packing, and, as always, many things are going wrong. There are problems with the construction in the condo, which will not be completed when I move in; several things I ordered, like light fixtures, we just discovered are discontinued; and one of my children is having difficulties. However, I know that if I can survive such an unbalanced time with some semblance of sanity, YOU CAN, TOO, and I hope the ideas in the book will help you. Remember, this, too, shall pass!

Warmly,

Barbara

PREFACE

Employees want to have the flexibility to deal with family needs on a day-to-day basis, as well as in an emergency. Companies are winning the loyalty of employees who get the work done, wherever and whenever they do their jobs.

Carol Evans, CEO of Working Mother Media

A STUDY TITLED *Workplace Trends: America's Attitudes About Work, Employers, and Government* found that 95 percent of working adults say they are concerned about spending more time with their immediate family and 92 percent say they want more flexibility in their work schedules to take care of family needs. The balance of work and family has become one of the top concerns for everyone in corporate America.[1]

We now have the highest percentage ever of women working outside of the home, and nearly one quarter of all households in America are headed by single parents. People must work longer and harder simply to stay even in today's economy, and more and more families are falling apart because of strained relationships, stress, and lack of quality time. Interestingly, younger workers value time with their families more than money, a fairly new phenomenon in American culture.

For most of us, the word *balance* immediately engenders feelings of guilt. The simple truth is that we will *never* be balanced in our lives at any one moment in time. Therefore, rather than worrying about balance, we need to look at our *whole* lives in terms of six areas of importance: **Work, Family, Friends, Health, Spirit,** and **Service.**

I often ask my audiences, "At age 18 in which of these areas did you invest the bulk of your time and energy?" The answer is always "Friends." Then I ask, "Where are you putting the bulk of your time and energy today?" Because most of the participants of my audiences are members of corporations, associations, or government organizations, they all answer "Work." Finally, I ask them to project to age 65 and consider where they think they'll invest the majority of their time and energy. The most frequent answers are "Health," "Family," or "Service." When we look at the whole spectrum of our lives rather than at any one slice in time, we begin to realize that "for everything, there is a season."

> All employees expect to have a life outside of work and smart employers recognize that.
>
> Ann Widman,
> spokesperson for
> Abbott Laboratories

In this book I'll introduce you to the concept of **BLENDING**. It begins with an acknowledgment of the area of your life where you are currently investing the bulk of your time and energy. Then, instead of berating yourself and feeling guilty for not being in balance, use that misguided energy to find creative ways to *blend* the other important areas of your life into that dominant area:

- *Work*/Family
- *Work*/Friends
- *Work*/Health
- *Work*/Spirit
- *Work*/Service

It's easier than you think! *Whether you are a human resources executive responsible for thousands of employees, or an employee worried about getting your own life in order,* this book will offer you dozens of creative, immediately applicable, no-cost or low-cost ideas to facilitate this blending. As a result, you can let go of guilt, relax with the idea that you are where you are supposed to be in life, and use your creative energy to find fun ways to blend all other aspects of your life into your dominant mode. You will then experience acceptance, a new enthusiasm, and a deeper sense of peace about the direction of your life.

Wherever you may find yourself in life, always remember:

1. You have CHOICES.
2. This, too, shall pass.
3. Blending involves lots of things coming together in different, creative ways, while balance is lateral, confining, guilt-producing, and judgmental.
4. Lighten up and find more joy and strive less for perfection in your life.

My hope is that the ideas in this book will touch your heart, stimulate your creative juices, make you smile, and, above all, banish forever the guilt that comes from thinking that you must do it all!

Barbara Glanz Communications, Inc.
<www.barbaraglanz.com>
bglanz@barbaraglanz.com
941-312-9169
Fax: 941-349-8209

ACKNOWLEDGMENTS

As YOU READ earlier, the time I have been writing this book has been one of the most stressful periods in my whole life, coming right after the loss of my husband and my move from a large home in Illinois to a smaller condo in Florida. I could not have accomplished what I have without many precious friends and colleagues.

Bonnie Michaels, an expert on work and family and a dear friend, not only spent time with me sharing ideas but also lugged a huge crate of her materials and books to my home as resources in my writing. She was available wherever her work and family took her, from Oregon to Florida, and I am so grateful for her help on this project.

Cindy Zigmund, the editor of this book, was the editor of my very first book in 1993, and we have been friends ever since. I was deeply touched when she, as the Publisher of Dearborn Trade, chose to be the one to edit this book. During the process she not only offered to help me pack, but she spent several afternoons working with me on the manuscript in progress to save me valuable time.

Mike Stewart, CSP, has been a dear friend and professional colleague. His advice, encouragement, and belief in me have kept me going when I was ready to give up. Sometimes, however, I didn't appreciate being told how "strong" I was!

A very special thank you goes to my "wonder-full" friend, John McPherson, the creator of the cartoon strip "Close to Home." His big heart and delightful sense of humor always brighten my days. He has so generously given me blanket permission to share his precious cartoons about family life with all of you. Thank you, John, for helping us to laugh at ourselves!

My Mastermind Group and precious friends in the Lord, John Blumberg, Manny Garza, and Joe Healey, have been there whenever I needed them. You will notice their contributions in this book.

Clyde Cawley is my only friend who is still up at 2 AM! He has been such a role model of courage and dignity as he fights his long battle with cancer, constantly reminding me of how small my troubles really are.

A very special thanks goes to all the dear friends who came over to help me pack so that I could write: Judy Constantino, Mary and Bud Verdi, Mike and Kirsten Goddard, and Laurie Trice helped pack family pictures, do fix-it jobs, sort, and get the house ready to be put on the market. Lonnie Bone not only brought me all her leftover boxes but also supplied me with lunches and spent several days packing, even after her own recent move. Pam Burks and Jean Palmer Heck flew all the way from Indiana to spend the weekend helping me organize and pack. (Jean is quite a taskmaster!) Pam's late-night calls checking up on me meant a lot. John Blumberg, Cheryl Perlitz, and Rita and Bruce Emmett laughed and talked as much as they packed! Sondra Brunsting, who shares my love of dolls and dollhouses, helped pack those precious treasures.

Judy Gaylord brought me dinner, packed for two days, did my ironing, and even drove me to the airport when I left for my new home. Sally Winkler, who packed up my pantry, and Diane Pedersen had a "picnic" lunch with me on the floor amidst all the boxes when there was no place to sit! Sue Brown, my former pastor's wife, cleaned out my junk drawer, and Penny Davoren tackled the medicine cabinet. Nancy Cobb brought lunch and stayed with me on the very emotional day the movers arrived. And last, special thanks to my precious new friend, Kim Rogers, who came over at 9:30 PM the last night before the movers came and stayed with me until 3 AM when we finally finished packing the last box, and showed up AGAIN the next morning at 7:30 to help guide the movers. Then, when the person who was going to handle my estate sale let me down at the last minute, Kim and her husband volunteered to take on this task as well. How very blessed I have been to have these wonderful friends!

All those other dear friends who wanted to help or are coming later to help UNPACK—Judy Ellsworth, Louanne Service, Shannon Johnston, Carol Jo DeFore, Karna Burkeen, Robin Maynard, Dan and Belle Fangmeyer, Scott and Melanie Gross, and my new assistant, Karen Wetherby—all of you are my "chosen" family.

Cathy and Renny Norman asked to host a "farewell" open house the Sunday before the manuscript was due. How I needed that affirmation and love at such a stressful, emotional time!

Bill Dunn, the contractor who oversaw the renovation of my new home in Florida when I could not be there—thank you for your expertise, honesty, and friendship. You made it possible for me to relax and write and not worry about what was happening down South!

And, finally, how grateful I am for my own family. I have been blessed with three wonderful children on earth and one in Heaven, with two children-in-love, and with two precious grandchildren. They are all constantly teaching me about blending and balance. How unbalanced my life would be without their love and support!

CONTENTS

INTRODUCTION

Out of the Pit and into the Blender

High achievers excel at making a living but often fail at making a life.

Jess O'Neil

DID YOU KNOW:

- Aon Consulting's *America@Work® Study 1998* found that of 17 factors that correlate significantly to workforce commitment, salary did not make the top 10. **The main thing employees said affected their commitment to their employer was "an employer's recognition of the importance of personal and family time."[1]**
- The Families and Work Institute (FWI) found that **88 percent of us say we work very hard, and that hard work causes negative spillover into the rest of our lives.** For example, 26 percent of American workers feel emotionally drained by their jobs, 28 per-

cent don't have energy to do things with family or others, and 36 percent just feel used up at the end of the day.[2]

- Young male workers, especially, highly value work-life benefits. A new Harris Poll showed that 7 in 10 would trade money for family time. According to an article titled "The 'family guy' lives: Young men will trade money for time" in the *Success in Recruiting and Retaining* newsletter, researchers at the Radcliffe Public Policy Center in Cambridge, Massachusetts, found the following: Eighty percent of men between the ages of 21 and 39 ranked family time at the top of the list of employee benefits they desire compared with 85 percent of women in the same age group. **Eighty-four percent of men and women in their 20s and 30s favored a family-friendly workplace above all other benefits.**

  Seventy-one percent of the men polled said they would gladly trade pay for more time with their families. This was true of 70 percent of 1,008 men in their 20s and 71 percent in their 30s, but only 26 percent of men over 65 agreed. **Four fifths of men ages 20 to 39 said having a work schedule that allows them to spend more time with family is more important than challenging work or a high salary.** And 63 percent of young women rated family time as more important than any other career factor.[3]

- A study titled *Workplace Trends: America's Attitudes about Work, Employers, and Government* found that **95 percent of working adults said they were concerned about spending more time with their immediate family,** and 92 percent said they want more flexibility in their work schedule to take care of family needs.[4]

- A survey commissioned by the Merck Family Fund titled *Yearning for Balance* found that people commonly said that three things would bring their lives more into balance and make their lives more satisfying:
  1. Spending more time with family and friends
  2. Reducing stress
  3. Doing more to make a difference in their communities[5]
- A *Hilton Generational Survey* quoted in *USA Today* reported the following concerns of the participants[6]:

Need more fun	68%
Need a long vacation	67%
Often feel stressed	66%
Feel time is crunched	60%
Want less work, more play	51%
Feel pressured to succeed	49%
Feel overwhelmed	48%

Why have I mentioned all these studies? To prove a point. **Workers today want a life!** Because of that need, this will be a very short book. My guess is that all of you who have chosen to read it are in the same situation—feeling periodically (or perhaps even daily) overwhelmed by guilt because you are NOT in balance, because you are desperately searching for ways to "do it all," and you simply are not succeeding. Just accept that you will probably NEVER lead a balanced life. Only when you accept this fact can you begin to let go of the guilt and learn some new, creative, fun, guiltbusting ways to integrate the various aspects of your life.

> **Bloom where you are planted.**
>
> An old saying from the 1960s

When we think about balance, the image of the scales comes to mind, symbolizing the idea that everything should be equal and in perfect symmetry. The reality is that none of our lives today is in perfect symmetry, and we feel out of control and guilty. Begin to think of your life in a long-term way, realizing that what is consuming you at one period of your life may become far less important at another stage.

The answer is to *recognize* where you are in your life today, *accept* that this is where you need to be right now, and then begin to *think creatively* about how to BLEND other aspects of your life into the one that is dominant. The concept implies there are very few parts of our lives that are completely separate. We take our home lives to work with us, and we take our worklives home. Our work and our family lives are affected by our health and our spirit. And I think we all inherently desire to be of service somewhere, sometime, in our lives.

The research is in—we all want more time with family and a more holistic lifestyle. This book will help stimulate your creative juices to

Work-life balance improves employee retention and yields much greater employee initiative and commitment. We know that it helps to reduce stress and burnout, and we are learning that it increases employee productivity . . . we can provide the tools for people to balance their lives, it's not up to management to do the actual balancing. Employees must take initiative to do that. We can't make the job easier, but we can add significant flexibility to the way our people work.

Lewis E. Platt, CEO, Hewlett-Packard Company

> I'm constantly amazed by the number of people who can't seem to control their own schedules. Over the years, I've had many executives come to me and say with pride: "Boy, last year I worked so hard that I didn't take any vacation." It's actually nothing to be proud of. I always feel like responding, "You dummy. You mean to tell me that you can take responsibility for an $80 million project and you can't plan two weeks out of the year to go off with your family and have some fun?"
>
> Lee Iacocca, *Iacocca, An Autobiography*

find *healthy* ways to incorporate other aspects of your life into your work-life, that part of your life where you are spending the bulk of your time and energy. We will do this in two ways:

1. Ideas that each INDIVIDUAL can adopt to create a more wholesome and satisfying life for himself or herself. Remember that having the option of CHOICE is power. You do not have to wait for management to create family-friendly policies and procedures. Rather, this book will show you that there are many things you can do to *be a catalyst* and make a difference in your own life.

2. Ideas that an ORGANIZATION can promote and champion in its work-life programs, management styles, and policies and procedures. These ideas will generally take more resources. However, they will demonstrate the seriousness with which an organization views its support of its employees. And in study after study, the findings reveal that when employee satisfaction with their work-life balance rises, financial results soon improve. In fact,

employees' satisfaction with their work-life balance was one of the two strongest predictors of customer satisfaction. That alone is reason enough to prove the value of the ideas that follow.

So, leave the guilt behind and get ready to jump into the blender!

1

A Foundation

My life is one. It encompasses all that I am: a corporate VP, a departmental manager, a wife, a daughter, a mother, and a grandmother. At the office, I fulfill personal as well as business responsibilities. I am much more productive when I live one life and when all things mesh. Reaching that point requires flexibility, organization, capable friends and colleagues, and lots of love.

A letter responding to a question about balance between work and life in Fast Company magazine, May 1999

IN THEIR BOOK *Living in Balance,* Joel and Michelle Levey share these thoughts:

If you're an average American adult, over a lifetime you'd spend approximately:
- *Five years waiting in line,*
- *Four years doing household chores,*
- *Three years in meetings,*

- *Six years waiting at red lights,*
- *One year watching TV commercials.*

Although many of us feel that all we do is work, if you are like the average person, your attention is specifically focused on work-related tasks for only about thirty hours a week, and you spend approximately ten or more hours a week doing things irrelevant to your job while you're at work, such as daydreaming or talking with co-workers about non-job-related things.

You spend nearly as much time—approximately twenty hours each week—with your attention turned toward leisure activities, with about seven hours in front of the television, three hours reading, two hours in activities like working out or playing music, and about seven hours in social activities with family and friends or going to parties or to entertainment. The remaining waking hours of your week are invested in basic maintenance activities such as commuting, eating, cooking, washing, shopping, puttering around, or in unstructured free time activities like just listening to music.[1]

Their suggestion is to bring more *mindfulness* to these everyday activities so that you become aware of how you are spending time and can recognize when you are out of balance. Then you will be able to come back into balance because your mind notices what is happening. They say as you practice more and more mindfulness, bringing alive the "here and now," you will stop falling off the tightrope—or at least you will be aware of falling and can figure out how to get back on. CHOICE FOLLOWS AWARENESS!

They go on:

Once we begin to cultivate mindfulness, we can reclaim our life from the sinkholes of regret about doing things we really didn't want to be doing but were too unaware to realize it at the time: missed opportunities, escalating problems, and dangerous accidents. By reclaiming the time and energy lost in these ways, mindful living is like having an extended "quality of life" policy![2]

The most important thing about mindful living is truly understanding that we have choices. I speak and write a great deal about choice because many people in our world today feel as if they are victims. They blame others or circumstances for their lots in life, and they do not take accountability to make changes. As a result, they lead lives of quiet desperation, feeling totally out of control and vulnerable.

Several years ago I created a visual model to help me and my audiences clearly understand the choices we have to make a difference in this world. This simple three-column chart illustrates that in any interaction, we have three choices: We can either create for that other person a minus, a zero, or a plus. If we discount them and make them feel less important than us or our organization, they will leave with a minus. If we simply take care of the immediate business at hand, they will leave with a zero because we have not created a relationship. However, if we make a human-level connection, then that person will leave feeling better because they interacted

> **The presence of guilt is not a result of making the wrong choice but of choosing itself. And that is the human condition: You are a being that chooses.**
>
> Peter Koestenbaum,
> *Fast Company*
> magazine, March 2000

with us. Recognizing someone as a human being with worth and value is the greatest gift we can give to a person. Remembering this both in your workplace and in your home will create a new spirit of caring and joy.

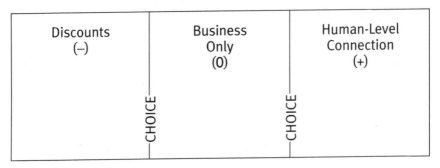

Your Choice in Any Interaction © Barbara Glanz Communications, Inc.[3]

In his book *Man's Search for Meaning,* Victor Frankl tells about his time in the concentration camps in World War II. Everyone in the camps is in the same circumstances—starving, ill, afraid, separated from home and family. However, some people in those circumstances became saints and would give their last crust of bread to a dying person. Others in the very same circumstances became swine and would rip the bread out of the dying person's mouth because he or she couldn't fight back. Frankl concluded that we cannot control most of our circumstances, but what we can *always* control is our response to them.

> The choice we offer people is what creates accountability.
>
> Peter Block,
> *Stewardship—Choosing Service Over Self-Interest*

The whole concept of choice is the most empowering gift you can give to another person. Once you understand in the deepest part of your being that you do have choices, then you have gained control over your life. Often after I conduct a workshop or deliver a keynote speech, people in my audiences will come up to me and say, "How can you smile all the time and how can you be so happy? You must have a perfect life!"

> To me, all the popular talk about "balance" was rubbish. There's no such thing as work-life balance if you can't get enough of both work AND life.
>
> Robert B. Reich

Well, I do not have a perfect life, and I suspect that neither do any of my readers. As mentioned earlier, my husband recently died of cancer, and we had a child who died. Suffice it to say I have experienced a great deal of pain in my life, but I CHOOSE TO BE A HAPPY PERSON, and you have that very same choice. No matter how difficult you find it to balance work and home, you always have choices, and the more aware you become of those choices, the more peace and control you will have over your life.

2

Understanding and Clarifying the Different Facets of Our Lives: Work, Family, Friends, Health, Spirit, and Service

Balance is an illusion—and to have it as a goal is self-defeating.

Melinda Brown, Vice President and General Counsel,
Lotus Development Corporation

As WE THINK about our whole lives, six distinct facets come to mind: Work, Family, Friends, Health, Spirit, and Service. For the purposes of this book, we will define each of the six areas this way:

WORK

Work is love made visible.

Kahlil Gibran

Your work is wherever you find your vocation. It may be in an office, at school, or at home.

Determined to increase productivity, management finds a way for employees to work straight through lunch.

> "Balance" has been the buzzword for so long it deserves to be enshrined in the Personal Goals and Objectives Hall of Fame. Actually, I consider myself a balance expert—a "balancing trying expert" to be more precise. I've researched and lived the balancing trauma for years and still double-book myself and eat microwave popcorn for dinner. The longer I try to balance, the more I learn that things feel and work better when I blend my life instead of trying to put things in cubbyholes or stack them up equally on different sides of the scale.
>
> Julie Danis

FAMILY

No matter who we are, we begin and end with family. The work will wait while you show your child the rainbow, but the rainbow won't wait while you do the work.

Patricia Clafford

When you put in place things that make employees' lives easier, you have much happier employees. In turn, we earn their loyalty.

Barbara Ashby, Manager of Child Care and
Family Services, University of California–Davis

I think most of us are blessed with three kinds of family:
1. Our *immediate family*, the people we live with and interact with each day

CLOSE TO HOME   JOHN McPHERSON

Hoping to convince management to provide a day-care center, employees at Gormley Industries staged a whine-in.

2. Our *extended family*, those relatives who do not live with us, some of whom we may only see at family reunions, but who are a part of our history

3. Our *chosen family*, in some ways the best kind of family members because they have come to us by choice, not by blood. In my family, Aunt Paula was one of those very special people, and she will always be remembered as an important part of the family.

FRIENDS

In the steady and merciless increase of occupations, the augmented speed at which we are always trying to live, the crowding of each day with more work than it can profitably hold, has cost us, among other good things, the undisturbed enjoyment of friends. Friendship takes time, and we have no time to give it.

Agnes Repplier, U.S. essayist

Friends are people you make a part of your life just because you feel like it.

Frederick Buechner

Two are better than one, because they have a good return for their work: If one falls down, his friend can help him up. But pity the man who falls down and has no one to help him up!

Ecclesiastes 4:9–10

We are all travelers in the wilderness of this world, and the best that we find in our travels is an honest friend.

Samuel Johnson

We have two basic kinds of friends, although they may certainly overlap:

1. *Personal friends*—those friends who are social friends, and
2. *Professional friends*—those friends with whom we work or with whom we share a work-related association.

HEALTH

*People need joy quite as much as they need clothing. Some of them need it
far more.*

Margaret Collier Graham

**Clepman Industries decided to make an example of
anyone who abused the sick-leave system.**

When I discuss health in this book, I am referring to both *physical* and *mental* health. These would include recreation and fun, exercise, and support/sharing groups.

SPIRIT

Work can provide the opportunity for spiritual and personal, as well as financial, growth. If it doesn't, then we're wasting too much of our lives on it.

James Autry, *Love and Profit—*
The Art of Caring Leadership

It is essential that everyone find new ways to break away from work at work and savor even a minute's reprieve from the rush and roar of the daily grind. This is one way to begin bringing a revitalized sense of being home for a few minutes wherever you happen to be, even at work.

Robert K. Cooper and Ayman Sawaf, *Executive EQ*

Spirit encompasses several aspects of our lives:
- Our spiritual or religious life or our deepest belief system
- Our avocation, what we love that we do not do for money, our "calling" For some fortunate people, their vocation may also be their avocation.
- Our hobbies and interests, those skills and talents that make us unique
- Our need for personal growth and development
- Our desire for continuing education or lifelong learning, without which our spirits become stagnant

- Our wish to find joy in our daily lives and a deeper reason for being
- Our need for recreation and fun

SERVICE

The only ones among us who will be truly happy are those who will have sought and found how to serve.

Albert Schweitzer

It's early Saturday morning and I have been up long before sunrise. I am in my office working because I have said "Yes" too many times when I should have said "No." I have had too many out-of-town trips, too many commitments to clients, too many projects, and, yes, too much NSA [National Speakers Association] work. I have given one of the best presentations of my career and one of the worst . . . all in a two-week time span. I have taught a class on Life Balance at my church and am writing an article as well. Yet, I have been out of connection with my family, my faith, my friends, and myself. I have lost 12 pounds that I didn't need to lose. I have had my planner, my laptop, and my luggage stolen. I have written this article twice on two different laptops. I am out of balance and that fact affects everything in my life. I am living the opening line from Charles Dickens *A Tale of Two Cities*—"It was the best of times, it was the worst of times, . . ."

Tim Richardson, professional speaker

There are several areas in which we can serve:

- Our family and friends
- Our profession
- Our community
- Our world

Notice that the areas of Health and Spirit are in-focused, stressing how important it is to take care of ourselves. Family, Friends, and Service, however, are all out-focused, encouraging service to others. Work is the only area of our lives that truly encompasses both (balance). It is in-focused when we are concentrating on personal growth and development, education, and fun. Yet it becomes out-focused when we think of our interactions with colleagues, friends, and the world outside our doors, the purpose and mission of the important difference our work is making, and the material advantages our work allows our families to have.

> When everything has its proper place in our minds, we are able to stand in equilibirium with the rest of the world.
>
> Frederic Amiel

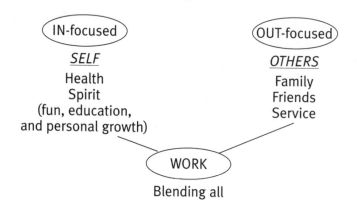

IN-focused   OUT-focused

SELF   *OTHERS*

Health   Family
Spirit   Friends
(fun, education,   Service
and personal growth)

WORK

Blending all

At different times in our lives we may find that we need to be more in-focused because of physical demands and the need to stay closer to home. As our family situations change, however, we often are able to expand our service horizons to wider and wider circles.

For now, think about that aspect of your life where you are spending the bulk of your time and energy. For most of us, that is at work, so for the rest of this book, we will look at unique and interesting ways you can blend the other areas of your life into your worklife.

One of the most exciting things about this whole concept of blending areas of our lives is the creativity we can experience while at the same time assuaging our guilt. Often we can blend two or even three areas of our lives together if we use our creative resources. H. Stanley Jones in his book, *Quality of Life—Achieving Balance in an Unbalanced World*, tells about an audience member who did just that! He excitedly told Dr. Jones how he had managed to find one activity that encompassed all the areas of his life:

My company (career) sponsored me in a Walk-A-Thon (health) for a local charity (community). I asked my wife to join me for companionship (family). She's a financial planner and during the course of the walk, she informed me about some new investment opportunities she thought we should take advantage of (financial). Of course, I enjoyed spending time with my wife during this event (leisure). The walk was quite a bit longer than I am accustomed to, but people were counting on me, and I really felt as though some inner strength was sustaining me (spirituality).[1]

3

Blending Work and Family

Sometimes I get so worn out being useful that I get useless.

Jan Karon, *At Home in Mitford*

LET'S START WITH the big one first. How many of you feel guilty because you are not finding enough time to be with your family? Baxter Labs recently completed a long-term global study in which they found that what their employees worldwide wanted most was "to be respected as whole human beings with a life outside of work." With all the changes in today's workplaces, it seems that most of us are constantly struggling to balance work and family. People are working longer hours, doing more with less, and finding themselves stretched to their very limits by the demands of their jobs. Little time and energy is left for family, and the organizations that encourage and support work-life initiatives are still few and far between.[1]

One of the answers to this crisis is to find creative ways to blend work and family. Let's look at dozens of ways individuals and families all over the world are creating more caring, joyful places to live whether they are single people, single parents, blended families, extended families, or retired families.

INDIVIDUAL IDEAS

My family doesn't interrupt my business. My business interrupts my family.

Art Berg, professional speaker

A *Fast Company* article titled "How Much Is Enough?" presented these interesting findings:

- Ninety-one percent of employees surveyed said that making personal life more of a priority was very important.
- Seventy-seven percent related that if money were not an issue, they would either quit work or reduce their hours.
- Fifty percent reported that they have no control over how many hours they work.[2]

> We are always too busy for our children; we never give them the time or interest they deserve. We lavish gifts upon them, but the most precious gift—our personal association, which means so much to them—we give grudgingly.
>
> Mark Twain

What telling statistics to support how important it is to find ways to blend work and family!

Share your work with your family. Research shows that one of the things employees want is a "feeling of being in on things." Family members want the same thing—to be a part of one another's lives outside of the home. That is why parents often annoy their children by constantly asking, "What happened at school today?" The exciting news is that there are many fun and interesting ways to involve your family in your work, and when that happens, you'll be surprised at how much more willing they are to include you in their lives as well.

Manny Garza, the president and founder of Manny Garza Encouragement Ministries, Spring, Texas, recounts the effects sharing his work with his family has had on his daughter:

> **Your children need your presence more than your presents.**
>
> Jesse Jackson

The impact of constantly finding ways to include my 11-year-old daughter, Jordon, in projects for the ministry we operate has affected her more than her mother and I realized. One day recently we discovered that she had formed her own ministry. She had produced her own business cards on her computer. She also made a poster describing her ministry, demonstrating a clarity of vision that could be an example to businesses everywhere! She named her ministry "One Step Closer—We help you get closer to God." She even described how she got started, giving me the credit for something I didn't even know I had done. It just impressed me so powerfully that sometimes the greatest influence we have in our children's lives comes not so much from our words as from our including them in the activities of our work.

"My baby-sitter's got the flu."

Videotape the place where you work. Do a "walking tour" showing where you park in the morning, where you enter the building and what it looks like on the outside, the reception area if you have one, the cafeteria or break room where you have lunch each day, and, most important, your office, cubicle, or work area. (Make sure you have a family picture and family mementos VISIBLE in your work space.) Include "Hellos" from some of your colleagues if you feel comfortable.

Invite your family members, perhaps one at a time, to join you for lunch. Some parents allow their children to each have a special "Dad or Mom" (or Grandpa/Grandma, Aunt/Uncle) day when they get to take a day off from school to visit their family member's workplace. Don't forget to invite your parents, too. No matter what their age, they will be thrilled to see what you have accomplished in your work.

Give your family members logo gifts from your organization. This makes them feel that they are a part of your worklife. By creating a feeling of partnership with your family, you help prevent any twinges of jealousy that you care more about your job than you do about them. Also they will enjoy the pride that comes from advertising "their" favorite organization.

Ask your family members to help you with a work project. It may be as simple as stuffing envelopes, or stapling papers, or filing and sorting; however, if the project is worked on as a family, it creates closeness rather than a feeling of separation. Little children can put stamps on envelopes while older children input basic information into the computer. Then plan some type of celebration as a reward at the end of the task. My family members are very involved in my work as a professional speaker and author. My daughter Erin creates all the bright-colored, laminated flip charts I post around the room or ballroom whenever I speak. My daughter Gretchen creates the wonderful slides I use in my presentations, and her husband Randy is my Webmaster. My son Garrett at one time was involved in selling my books, and my husband Charlie often traveled with me and kept my financial records. It has become "our" business!

John Blumberg, a professional speaker from Naperville, Illinois, shared with me how he and his son, Ryan, found a fun and creative way to blend work and family:

> Put your calendar where your mouth is: Schedule your family time. What's left is work or playtime.
>
> Anthony Robbins

My 14-year-old son, Ryan, had been attending the National Speakers Association's national convention with me since he was 10. It had become an annual tradition for the two of us and we both looked forward to it. Ryan loved attending the Youth Leadership Conference, while I attended the "adult" version of the convention! Each night we enjoyed comparing stories of our day's activities in our hotel room.

Now attending the convention for his fifth year, Ryan has become increasingly aware of all aspects of this annual event. We were sitting and waiting for the 7 AM NSA-style Sunday Mass to begin. It was early, and we had been up late, but Ryan was already watching. He leaned over and asked why some people had orange name tags. I told him that those were given to speakers who had obtained their Certified Speaking Professional (CSP) designation, a significant designation within NSA that is earned by the speaker. I knew what Ryan's next question would be: "When are you going to get an orange name tag?" My automatic pilot responded, "Soon." The next logical question was "How soon?"

I then explained all the paperwork and data collection that you had to do to complete the application. It isn't difficult, but it does take time. It was then that I saw the application challenge as an opportunity. And so I asked him a question, "Do you want to help me get that orange tag?" He didn't hesitate, "Sure!"

Within a week of returning from the convention, we picked a couple of nights to work on making a list of all the presentations I had done. I had fortunately kept one envelope for every speaking engagement with all the details inside the envelope. It would have been a huge chore going through this data gathering by myself, but with Ryan, it turned into an interesting project. As we listed the events, he would ask questions about many of them. It was fun to reflect on each of those audiences and experiences, and I know Ryan has a greater insight into what I do as a result of our working together. It was the perfect opportunity to blend work and family—and turn a chore into a JOY in the process!

 Don't forget parents or other elders. Often our parents or older relatives have no idea what we do, so finding ways to include them in your work not only can help you but can also bring them great joy. Invite them to lunch if they live close or are visiting and introduce them to your coworkers and boss. Even if they live at a distance, you can find creative ways to involve them in your work such as asking them to research a project for you at the library or watch for articles on a subject that relates to your work.

Organic, a Web-design and e-services firm in New York City, held a *"Bring Your Parents to Work Day"* to help parents learn what their Web-obsessed kids actually do for a living. The first event was a talk show during which the parents did their best to explain what they thought their children do. Then they were told what their children really do and why. After enjoying pizza, the employees checked back in with their parents who now finally understood more about their children's careers. What a wonderful way to promote intergenerational understanding and communication!

♥ *Bring home articles about your work, pictures of your boss and coworkers, and samples of your marketing materials.* If you help to create a product, bring home examples to show your family. Children also love the little gimmicky things often given out at trade shows or obtained from vendors. When you bring these items home, they know that you were thinking of them.

♥ *Show a video of projects that you are working on to your family.* The more they feel involved in your worklife, the more understanding they will be when you have to stay late or work on weekends.

♥ *When you receive an award at work, make sure you share it with your family.* Invite them to the ceremony if possible. If it's monetary, share it with each family member—go on an outing of some kind or buy a gift that you have all been wanting. You might even hold a family conference to decide, with each family member having a vote. Let them really know that you couldn't have done this without their support.

♥ *When you are involved in a long project, give your family a calendar.* This way, they know the exact extent of your commitment. Each night at the dinner table they can check off a day, and you can report on your progress. This way, even if your project is spread over several months, they can see an end in sight and also feel a part of the process. (This idea works especially well if you have to travel. Color-code the travel days on the calendar, especially for young children, so that everyone knows what to expect and can plan around your schedule. They can also check off the days to visualize how long it will be until you return.) Use fun stickers to mark special points of progress or accomplishments along the way. And don't forget to celebrate THE END!

 Invite family members to help with a project at the office. Burns Smith from Nationwide Insurance, Knoxville, Tennessee, told me about one of the most memorable days his sons and youngest daughter have ever had. One Saturday morning he brought them to work with him. The company had decided to dispose of a large pile of old videotapes, so Smith took the children to the conference room, gave them the tapes and a couple of hammers, and told them to destroy the tapes in any way they'd like. He said they worked for several hours, pounding the tapes, jumping on them, and strewing film they had pulled out all over the room. He says they STILL talk about that day many years later! Another person shared how she brought her children into the office on the weekend after a business trip. They helped her sort her "in" box to prepare for Monday morning.

Lorraine Harris, a county health human resources manager, says, "Periodically, I take my ten-year-old daughter to work and have her do *light typing, photocopying, sorting papers,* etc. We discuss different events that occur in my job and how they relate to things she does at school, such as comparing performance appraisals I do with report cards that she gets."

Kha Thomas-Williams, the Assistant City Manager of Thomasville, Georgia, has her daughter help *file* her human resources publications that accumulate all too quickly! She says, "Both my kids (8 and 11) help me set up meetings at off-site locations. They really like helping when the meetings are held at plantation locations because they get to see nature—the woods, lakes, and all the forest animals."

Karen Petkis of the Hartford Insurance Company had a *Power-Point presentation* to do, so she made a big bowl of popcorn and asked her 11-year-old son, Stephen, to help. He surprised her by creating some wonderful slides using the image of a house and adding accessories and other objects as the presentation went on. He ended up having fun doing the whole presentation, Karen didn't waste her weekend with something she wasn't good at, and the people to whom she was presenting loved the story of the "family affair"!

 Give your family members your business cards to share with their friends and acquaintances. This lets them share in your work and be proud of what you do for a living. Who knows, they might even send a new customer your way! You might want to have some special business cards made with a picture of your family on the back. So often the business cards I see are blank on the back, missing a wonderful opportunity to communicate something more than just the business identity of the person. By including a family picture on the back, you make a human-level connection with the receiver that will be much more memorable than just receiving a standard business card. It also demonstrates the importance of your family in your life. Of course, you must check your organization's policy on business cards first, but this might be a time to encourage a change!

 Take family members to conferences with you. As described earlier, John Blumberg has taken his son Ryan with him to the National Speakers Association convention for the past five years. Ryan tells his version of the benefits:

These past five years at the NSA convention have been a great time for my Dad and me. In the morning, we visit and then he drops me off at the youth part of the convention and he goes to the adult sessions. At our Leadership Conference we play games and listen to really cool and interesting speakers. You meet a lot of people your age and make many new friends. Everyone is really nice and the Youth Leadership Staff is a great group of older kids. When the day comes to an end, my Dad picks me up and we go back to our hotel room and talk about the highlights of our day. It is fun to sit back and relax and talk to each other about what we did that day. Our convention time-out on Monday night has been fun, too, for I get to tag along with Dad to dinner with the adults. I have met speakers from Illinois, Minnesota, and Ohio. They have all been really fun! The NSA Youth Leadership Conference is the highlight of my summer!

Most children, it seems, have no idea what their parents really do. However, John says that Ryan has started to understand the speaking business and has been able to actually live a part of it.

 Share computer ideas with your children. Show them the projects you are involved in at work. Dale Stefan of S&T Bank in Indiana, Pennsylvania, says, "You'd be surprised how well they respond because they are taught a lot of the same software at school." Bank employees are offered a computer purchase program through payroll deduction. Then the bank sponsors evening and weekend family personal computer classes.

Keep a drawer of your children's things—artwork, pictures, etc.—at work. Include special things for them to do when they come to visit as well. When the child comes to visit, he or she will feel connected to your work, and each time you open that drawer, you will feel connected to the child. You may also want to allocate a special chair in your office just for your family's use.

They will love it even more if you *display their artwork in your office* or if they find you using the clay dish, vase, or ashtray they made. You might even make it a point to wear whatever "jewels" your child has made or bought for you. For years Ed Burkeen, a very special friend of ours, kept a small picture frame that our daughter, Erin, made for him from Popsicle sticks one Christmas. He said it reminded him that she was the only baby who didn't cry when he picked her up, and she loved knowing that it was always there on his desk!

Mail something to your child (or wife or husband or significant other) from work. This might be a cartoon, a card, a small book, a fancy pencil, or even a candy bar. Your child (or other family member) will be surprised and especially delighted that you were thinking of them during your workday.

♥ *Hold family meetings at dinnertime when everyone shares what they did that was good at their "work" that day.* Help children and spouses understand that their "work," whatever it may be (going to school, running a home, volunteering in the community), is just as important as yours is.

♥ *Celebrate with the family when a big project is completed.* Even if your family was not directly involved, they certainly were affected by your working extra hours, so plan a special celebration when the big project ends to thank them for supporting you.

♥ *Work at home at least a few days a month so that your family can really "see" what you do.* This will also allow you time to participate in the activities that are important to them. In your home office, whether it is used part-time or full-time, keep a sign on your door that says "Open" and "Closed." When the clock strikes closing time, put the sign out, shut the door, and LEAVE.

Manny Garza, the founder and President of Encouragement Ministries, shares the way he involves his family from his home office:

I work from a home office in Spring, Texas, and keeping the "door open" to the family is important to me. One of the ways I have involved my 11-year-old daughter, Jordon, is by always asking her opinion on any graphic work or marketing materials we produce. Her first response to copy and colors is incredibly perceptive. If the message doesn't reach an 11-year-old child, it won't reach anyone! And because she has overheard me telling others how much I value her opinion, her sense of contribu-

tion and pride have skyrocketed. One of our key pieces even contains her words as the main point!

Manny also says he always tapes the lessons he teaches and Jordon helps him duplicate them, another shared "business" task.

 If you are moving into a new work space or office, have your family come in on the weekend or in the evenings to help you set up. They will feel a part of the move and experience firsthand where you will be each day. Helping you provides a special kind of team-building experience and also lets them feel a part of your whole life.

 Invite your retired parents to help you at work. Nothing makes a parent prouder than to see how successful and well respected their son or daughter is at work. Many organizations could use volunteers for such jobs as greeters and guides, and retired folks need to be needed.

Being an effective single parent, according to George Walther, CSP, CPAE, a professional speaker from Seattle, Washington, boils down to this:

If you choose to be an effective parent, you must accept fewer speeches, reduce overnight travel, consider your child's school performances and family celebrations as "booked dates," and adjust your

> **Anybody who is logging hours to impress me, you are wasting your life. Get the work done and then go home to your families.**
>
> Colin Powell, then Secretary of State

office schedule so that it minimally conflicts with your parenting time. That's really all there is to it.

Tactically, here's how I've decided to balance my profession and my parenting. When I first became a daddy, I closed my big, impressive downtown headquarters and added office space to my home. Now, here is my daily at-home schedule:

I arise very early, between 4 and 5 AM, and work in my home office while Kelcie sleeps until 7 AM. From 7 to 9 I'm on Dad duty with Kelcie. After we eat breakfast and complete schoolwork together, I walk with my daughter to the bus stop and chat with the other parents and kids. When the school bus pulls away, I return to my home office. At 3:44 PM I walk to the bus stop and welcome my child home. I don't work in the evenings. I parent.

Once a week, I volunteer to work in my daughter's classroom. After five years of consistently volunteering, all the kids know me, and my daughter is proud to have her daddy work at her school. Every teacher knows that I'm a dedicated parent and that I'll do anything from writing a PTA check to serving as moderator at the school's annual Geography Bee to acting as auctioneer at the school fundraiser.

Although I have reduced my speaking schedule, I still travel. When I'm away, Kelcie sleeps over at one of her friends' homes. I make sure that her friends come for sleepovers at our house often enough that the ledger of parents helping each other is never out of balance.

When I travel to speaking engagements, my home phone is set to "call forward if busy" to my mobile phone. When I head for the airport, I take the home phone off the hook so that it busies out. The school, our neighbors, or Kelcie can dial my local home number and the call will immediately forward to my mobile phone wherever I am. Kelcie knows *she can easily reach me, and she also knows that I'll phone her each morning before she goes to the school bus stop.*

I can work more later in my career. I'm grateful to have a comfortable life, my clients can count on having a happy, healthy, sane speaker show up in front of their audiences, and, most important, my daughter and I both benefit from having a satisfying, loving relationship.

Communicate with your family in creative ways from work or on the road

Call home and leave a voice-mail message to let your loved ones know you were thinking of them.

Send e-mail messages to your family members. Now that it is easy to get your e-mail on the road, this can be done both from the office and when you are traveling. Just a quick note to let spouses, significant others, or children know what is going on in your world will keep them connected.

Liz Curtis Higgs, a professional speaker who travels 30 weekends per year, always makes a *phone appointment with her family every night.* This is the time they all keep up on what is happening in one another's lives.

Another speaker takes a digital camera with him on every business trip. He *takes pictures of the place he is speaking and e-mails them home every night.*

◆ Jolene Brown, a professional speaker from West Branch, Iowa, has been greeted *by faxes from her children waiting at the hotel.* I love that the speaker's family takes the initiative to make her feel missed and loved!

◆ Jeff Blackman, a consultant from Glenview, Illinois, *hides Post-it notes all over the house* for his wife and children to find when he is on a business trip.

◆ *Buy two identical books written at your child's age level.* On one or more nights of the week that you are traveling, call your child just before bedtime and read to your child his or her "night-night" story. You will have one copy of the book and your child will have the other, so he or she can read along with you. If you have more than one child, read to each child on a separate phone. This practice will make them feel as if you have really "tucked them in"!

◆ *Recording*—I love this story from the book *Cancer: A Gift of Life* by Clyde C. Cawley:

Throughout my entire cancer experience, I never lost my voice. So one day I asked the children's minister at church if it would be appropriate to record children's books for use in her Sunday School ministry. She thought it to be a good idea, so I bought an inexpensive tape recorder, a few inexpensive children's books and began to record. We tested a few books with good results—the children seemed to enjoy listening to the tape and reading along with the book in front of them.

Being from a corporate background, however, I realized I needed to get copyright clearances from the publishers to continue the project. I

"Be sure to compliment him on his wife and kids."

wasn't certain it was worth the effort to continue the project, so one day I came into the room and was introduced as the person whose voice was on the recordings. The teacher asked me to read the children a story. I sat on the floor while eight children gathered around to see the book and the pictures. We took a lot of time to read through the book because I asked a lot of questions as I read each page, and the children were quick to answer. We had a wonderful time interacting, so much so that I decided to volunteer to read in person rather than continue recording the books on tape.

Later, I reflected on my own children's upbringing. I realized how often I had missed them while traveling on corporate business. I would call them but it was never the same as being with them in person. I never read to them (or so it seemed looking back on the experiences many years later), but they grew up with books all around them. If only I had recorded some of their books for them to enjoy while I was traveling, I thought. They could enjoy the sound of my voice reading to them as if I were there in person. What a gift! If only I had thought to do this simple thing.

If you are a traveler with children, why not take time to record some books for your children? They will enjoy your voice while you are away, and they will gain a love for reading that will benefit them forever. Then, why don't you volunteer to read to children at your church or charity location? Children need to become involved in reading. They need adult guidance. Why not combine the two and have a ball?

 Take your family with you. Joe Healey, a professional speaker and consultant from Virginia Beach, Virginia, found a unique way for his family to travel with him:

In 1996 my wife, Jill, and I decided to go outside the box to fulfill our desire to share more time and experiences together as a family. We have three children who at that time were ten, seven, and six. We decided to take advantage of the technology that the digital age is offering in the form of mobility. We moved into a 34-foot motor home where we lived, worked, schooled, and played for 18 months. We visited 44 states and had a grand adventure. Everyone had a blast, grew tremendously, and felt it surpassed our expectations in enriching us.

Even though this idea really is "outside the box," it could work for many people who are self-employed or might even trigger an idea for a sabbatical. If you want more information on the details of this adventure, you can contact joe@joehealey.com. *The point is—be creative!*

 Kris Thomson, a human resources manager for Jostens in Shelbyville, Tennessee, writes about *taking her family with her:* "I have tried to bring one or all of my family members with me to special places that I must travel to for work. My sons still talk about the times I took one to Las Vegas, or my other son to Orlando, or my whole family to San Diego. They plan what we'll do 'after work' and it's a special time for me to focus on them and have fun. Because of these experiences, they don't see my travel as a 'burden' or regret my need to be gone."

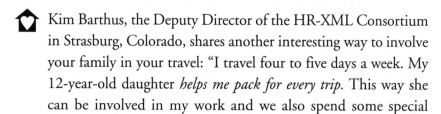

Kim Barthus, the Deputy Director of the HR-XML Consortium in Strasburg, Colorado, shares another interesting way to involve your family in your travel: "I travel four to five days a week. My 12-year-old daughter *helps me pack for every trip*. This way she can be involved in my work and we also spend some special together time before I leave."

La Petite Academy is now offering an innovative service called the *Kids Station Passport Program* to parents whose jobs require travel. This is available to all parents whether their children are enrolled in a La Petite Academy or not. Parents can now take their children on their business trips with them by reserving space at a La Petite Academy in their destination city. Reservations can be made online at <www.lapetite.com>.

Share your family with your coworkers and customers

Include a picture of your family on letters to longtime or favorite customers. Then let your family know you have done this. This will not only please your family, but it will help to create lasting, human-level relationships with your customers.

Invite colleagues to your home, particularly the person you report to, so that your family members can get to know them. If you are a manager, one of the most memorable things you could do would be to invite the families of your employees to your home. When I worked at Kaset International, a Times Mirror training company, the owners of the company invited all the families to their homes once a year. That gesture created more loyalty to the company and harmony at home than any monetary bonus they could have given!

Find special ways to include your family when you travel. If your work involves travel, you must try especially hard to involve your family. The more ways you can find to share travel with your family, the closer you will be and the more you will learn and grow together. Here are some creative ways to include your family in your business trips:

 Create "leave-taking rituals" to help kids feel more connected. Ask them to help you pack. Create fun geography quizzes on the cities you visit. Encourage kids to fax you their homework or drawings. Get them an e-mail address. When her children were younger, Liz Curtis Higgs, a well-known author, *laid out her children's clothes for each day she would be gone.* That helped them to experience a sense of her love and presence even when she was on the road. Another businessperson who likes to have fun with her children puts on her brightest lipstick and if the children are asleep when she is leaving or returning, she *tiptoes in and kisses them on the cheek.* In the morning when they awake, they laugh and laugh at the kiss marks left in the night!

Start a shadow box for each family member. When I began traveling in my speaking and consulting business, my sister gave each of my children a printer's drawer, that is, a shadow box. I did not want to get in the habit of bringing them big, expensive presents every time I was away, so I carried on a family tradition that my sister had started on her travels. Each time I travel, I bring each of my children some little thing that is a symbol of the city or country I visited—a miniature cable car from San Francisco, a little basket of tiny crabs from Maryland, a totem pole from British Columbia, a miniature bottle of Coke from Atlanta, a gavel from the U.S. Supreme Court in Washington, D.C., a little pineapple from Hawaii, a lighthouse from Rhode Island, a miniature jazz player from New Orleans, a tiny record from Nashville, a milk can from Wisconsin, a cowbell from Liechtenstein, a miniature Saint Bernard from Switzerland, a panda from San Diego, a duck from Memphis, and a small container of Vegemite from New Zealand! These gifts are fun to find, inexpensive, and easy to tuck into the corner of a suitcase, AND the children are learning special things about other cultures and parts of the country. Now my children are bringing souvenirs for the shadow box from their own trips!

 Give each family member a "Things to Tell Mom/Dad/Grandpa/ Grandma" notebook. To help keep in close touch with my children when I had to travel, I gave them a "Things to Tell Mom" notebook. I picked a special notebook for each of the girls that I knew they would like (our son was away for his first year of college). Then I told them to keep that notebook with them every day and write down anything they wanted to tell me. Every night when I called home, they would have their notebook lists as a reminder of what had happened during the day. I think they told me more because of those notebooks than they would have if I had been at home!

♥ *Purchase a large map and buy pins with colored heads.* Place pins in the cities you will be visiting on your trips so the children can see where you will be and all the different places you have traveled. If both parents travel, use one color for each parent. Then use another color for family trips.

♥ Liz Curtis Higgs, a professional speaker from Louisville, Kentucky, enjoys *studying a map* with her children before she leaves on a business trip so they will know visually where their Mom is going. This is also a wonderful way for them to learn geography.

♥ When you return, *share with them special things about the area you visited* (even if YOU never got out of a hotel room or an office!). A businessperson I know says he always *remembers two things* that are unique to the place he has traveled. Then when he returns, he and the children play a game called Name Two Things. This allows him to teach them about interesting areas and unusual facts about these areas.

♥ *Surprise family members with little things* to let them know you are thinking about them. Bonnie Michaels, president of Manag-

ing Work and Family in Evanston, Illinois, shares a new family ritual she and her husband have created to help them feel close to
each other when traveling:

*When I go away, I leave a special note for him under his pillow. When
he goes away, I leave a special note for him in his suitcase. He does the
same for me. In addition, he has left poems on my e-mail or special
messages on my voice-mail. All these little gestures help the traveler feel
special and connected, appreciated and cared for.*

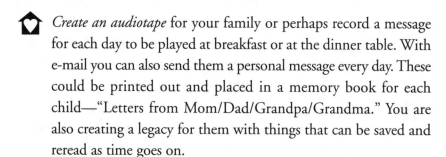

Create an audiotape for your family or perhaps record a message
for each day to be played at breakfast or at the dinner table. With
e-mail you can also send them a personal message every day. These
could be printed out and placed in a memory book for each
child—"Letters from Mom/Dad/Grandpa/Grandma." You are
also creating a legacy for them with things that can be saved and
reread as time goes on.

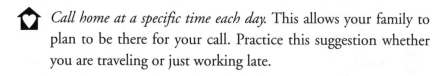

Call home at a specific time each day. This allows your family to
plan to be there for your call. Practice this suggestion whether
you are traveling or just working late.

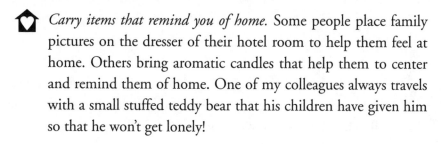

Carry items that remind you of home. Some people place family
pictures on the dresser of their hotel room to help them feel at
home. Others bring aromatic candles that help them to center
and remind them of home. One of my colleagues always travels
with a small stuffed teddy bear that his children have given him
so that he won't get lonely!

Save your frequent-flier miles to use for family travel. We were able to bring each of our children home for Thanksgiving when they were in college with my frequent-flier miles, a trip we could not have afforded otherwise. One of my colleagues lets each of her children choose one business trip a year to accompany her using her frequent-flier miles. This provides a special sharing time for both of them and memories that are irreplaceable! Another friend was able to take his whole family to Hawaii because of all the business travel he had done. Hanoch McCarty, coauthor of *Chicken Soup for the Grandparent's Soul,* as a single father committed to take his children on every third business trip he scheduled. Another businessperson has committed to taking his wife with him once a month and his children every three months.

 Extend weekends with family members at special travel destinations. Many organizations will pay for a hotel room for the weekend if you can show them that you save airfare by staying over a Saturday night. Then the trip becomes a minivacation for you and your family with only the cost of meals, and possibly airfare.

 Mail a love letter to your partner's destination when he or she takes a trip. This will let him or her know that you were missing your partner before he or she even left! It will also remind him or her of the person at home awaiting his or her return.

 Place a packet of "special" tissue in the person's suitcase. Pull out one tissue, write a message on it and stuff it back in the box. This one will REALLY surprise your partner!

Find special ways to share bedtime with your children while on the road. The Duchess of York tells how she keeps her children close when she travels:

Last Easter, I was in Argentina for ten days. So for every night I'd be gone, I left them a tape of an Easter story I read. I went through the Last Supper and then what Easter Sunday was all about. I would ask, "Now are you in your bed?"[3]

 When you can't be there for a special event, phone immediately to hear the details while they are still fresh in their minds. Always do your best to attend at your family's special events, but if you absolutely cannot, plan ahead if at all possible. Have them videotape or audiotape the event, and then as soon as you get home, sit down with them to experience it together.

 Share the culture, art, and history of the places you visit. Purchase books about the places you visit and share them with your family when you return. Through letters and family discussions, you can expose your children to the wonders of other parts of the world.

 Carry family pictures with you when you travel (and let your family know that you are doing this). Place them around your hotel room to help you feel more closely connected to your family. Most of us today are visual learners, so having photos in view has an important psychological impact. Also share your family's pictures with your clients and those with whom you travel. When I was conducting training throughout the United States, often for several days at a time, my children at home would always ask, "Have you shown your class our picture yet?" Hanoch McCarty shared with me an exercise he often does with an audience. He asks them to take out a picture of someone they love, share it with the person next to them, and tell what that person or persons means to them. What a great way to create immediate bonding!

 Take conference giveaways home to your children. Most conferences have expo centers where vendors display their wares. The vendors usually offer some type of giveaway to get you into their booths. When I speak at a conference, I love visiting the expo centers and collecting things like stuffed animals, silly pens, stress balls, and other fun items. Then I package them up and send them to my little four-year-old grandson, Gavin, in Seattle. He loves Granna Barbara's surprises, and I have fun collecting them for him.

 Rita Emmett, a speaker and author from Des Plaines, Illinois, tells about what she calls *"The Postcard Connection":*

Like many women, I'm on the road for business trips a great deal and never seem to have as much time as I'd like with our seven grandchildren. So I send them little "care packages" in the form of postcards.

I've set up my database so that all I have to do is push a button and a set of labels with all seven names and addresses pops out. When I arrive at my destination, one of the first things I do is find some great postcards, and it takes just seconds to put on the labels.

For the bigger guys, ten-year-old Kenny and seven-year-old Mike, I might put some educational fact such as "This is almost the biggest state in

*the United States. Do you know the name of the one state that is bigger?"
And for the little ones I might find a picture of a chipmunk or a riverboat
or a train and write a simple message about whatever is in the photo.*

*Or I'll let them know I'm thinking about the important things in
their lives. "Can't wait to hear about your swimming lesson," or "I'll
pray that you do well on your test this week." Sometimes I'll send them
all something silly: "I was on top of this mountain and saw Pokemon,"
or "Would you believe that I sneaked onto this rocket ship and went to
Jupiter and back?"*

*It seems that it doesn't matter WHAT I write, children of all ages love
receiving their very own mail. Several of the children have saved all the
postcards they've received and sometimes the cards generate discussions.
They'll ask me how a certain town was or did I really sneak onto a
rocket ship, or they'll tell me that when I was in New York, they saw a
show about New York that depicted the very same thing that was on my
postcard. It's a fun, easy way to have an extra connection with each of
them and just a simple way to let them know somebody cares a whole
bunch about them.*

 Paul Mallon, an executive with Dearborn Trade Publishing,
Chicago, Illinois, sends his grandson postcards from every place
he travels. That way Cameron knows where Grandpa is and a little more about what he does. This is an important way for them
to keep connected.

**Here are some travel tips to minimize the stress of business travel on
both the traveler and family.** Richard Leider, a Minneapolis-based
consultant on lifestyle management, suggests:

- Carefully analyze the purpose of each trip; say no to unnecessary ones. That's good for you, your family, and your business!
- Draw travel "boundaries" as a family, deciding how much travel is excessive.

CLOSE TO HOME   JOHN McPHERSON

"Eh, eh, eh! You know the rules!
No bugging Mom at work!"

- Maintain reasonable intervals between trips if possible.
- Don't travel on weekends, unless it's absolutely unavoidable.
- Don't travel on special occasions such as birthdays and anniversaries.
- Telephone home each day.
- Take an hour off on the road each day to be alone, relax, exercise, or do something new and different.
- Schedule weekly relationship time on your calendar.
- Take a loved one on business trips occasionally.
- When you come home, listen before you share the details of your journey.
- Write down a master dream list. List all the things you want to do, be, or have, or what you have going on in your lifetime. Make one dream come true each year with your family.[4]

Help your children develop and maintain a positive attitude about work. Most of us will spend the majority of our lives working, at jobs both paid and unpaid. It is important that we help our children feel good about our work and thus about working in general. Here are five suggestions to give our kids a positive attitude about work:

1. Select books to read about different jobs or professions. Richard Scarry's wordbooks are especially fun to read.
2. Tell your children what you do for a living in language they can understand.
3. When your children complain about the number of hours you work, remind them how they benefit by your working. Of course, the financial reward is a direct benefit, but you and your family gain from your experiences, the people you meet, the friends you make, and the places you travel.

4. Try not to always blame your crankiness or tiredness on work. Let them know that work can also be stimulating, uplifting, and satisfying.

5. Above all, try to make time for your children no matter how hard you work. Let them know that while you want to provide for them, they are more important than your job. Your children should never feel like they have to compete with your work.

Eat dinner together as a family. Although most of these ideas are quite simple, they will make a huge difference in how your family feels about your job because you have made them *sharing participants* in your work. Perhaps the most important idea is to try at least four nights a week to have dinner as a family. Do not just let dinner happen, but plan it so that it truly becomes a sharing time. One idea is to begin each week with a family commitment such as:

- We will each give five compliments to someone a day. OR
- We will each do something kind for someone else every day. OR
- We will each choose a new book to read this week. OR
- We will each write a note to thank someone this week. OR
- We will each find one funny thing that happened to us to share this week.

Then at dinner each night discuss your progress. One of the things we always shared in our family was what we had learned that day. If you gently plan and guide family conversation, you will indirectly provide opportunities to share one another's lives in a special way. All these activities will create memories, sharing, and the blending of work and family we so desperately need in our world today.

Look at how your career is affecting your family now, and also how it will five years from now. Every night and weekend that you work and every trip you take has a personal consequence. Have you thought about those consequences? Alan Zimmerman, Ph.D., CSP, tells this anecdote:

> *I remember in the early days of my speaking career, one of my daughters would often interrupt me when I was working on a program. She'd say, "Dad, Dad," and then ask a series of questions or want to do a variety of activities. More often than not, I'd say, "Not now . . . later . . . I'm busy . . . leave me alone." And eventually, she did. We had no relationship for several years.*
>
> *Time does pass more quickly than you think. You'll soon be facing the consequences of your present work decisions. So be sure you make those decisions in the context of how they will affect your personal and professional life.*

Join or start a committee to make changes in the organization to help it become more family-friendly. Don't simply wait for management to make desired changes, but be proactive. Help interested coworkers come together, research the topic area you would like to see changed, interview other companies who have model programs, find out costs involved, and, finally, present your findings to senior management in an organized and thoughtful way. Often management does care but simply does not choose to take the time to explore various options. Those who will be most affected by the changes should be the leaders of the movement. If you do the legwork, then it will be much more likely for these changes to actually occur.

Use the computer to blend work and home. In an article titled "The New Consciousness Raising" by Nancy Evans in *Working Woman* magazine, she says, "The computer's presence at work and at home has significant ramifications for women. It means we can do what we ultimate multitaskers have always wanted to do: blend our personal and professional lives. We can check out summer camps online during lunch and look into a work project over breakfast. The computer, it turns out, is a facilitator for blending. Who knew?"[5]

You can also share computer ideas with your children. When you are working on a project at work, bring a disk home and show your family how you are using the computer to accomplish the task at hand.

Practice "buffering." One of the ways multiple roles can help us enjoy a happier life is to consciously think about buffering. With buffering, if things aren't going well and you feel inadequate in one place, you often have the comfort of knowing that you're OK in the other. Family responsibilities can buffer the impact of negative events at work, and work can serve as a buffer for problems at home. An office manager with a two-year-old says, "It's hard to leave home in the morning and hard to leave work at night. I get so caught up in what I'm doing—I really enjoy both parts of my life." And Larry, a computer programmer, says, "Looking forward to seeing my family at night softens the impact of any negative things that happen during the day."

ORGANIZATIONAL IDEAS

The moral is simple: If you satisfy their deep wants, employees become more cognitively and emotionally engaged and will perform better. And this is so across national and corporate cultures, in all occupations, regardless of rates of pay, because the underlying needs are universal.

James K. Harter, *Taking Feedback to the Bottom Line*

A new survey by Hewitt Associates presents some key findings for benchmarking your organization. They found that

- 57 percent of employers surveyed offer flextime and 47 percent offer part-time employment.
- 90 percent of employers offer some type of childcare benefits to employees.
- 47 percent of employers offer eldercare assistance.
- 52 percent offer some type of on-site personal service to employees.
- 37 percent of employers provide financial security programs to help employees decide about their retirement and investments.
- 75 percent of employers provide employees with education opportunities.[6]

These programs are well worth the cost. Consider the following:

Prudential Insurance Company invested more than $1.4 million in their major work-life program, LifeWorks. But according to corporate officials, it was well worth it. Why? Because the effort generated almost $6 million in savings through enhanced attraction and retention efforts—nearly a 5-to-1 cost savings. The chief components of the program are: childcare referrals, eldercare referrals, adoption advice, and education referrals and advice. More than 10,000 employees have accessed these services.[7]

A survey of 70 companies found that every dollar spent on family resource programs yielded more than $2 on direct-cost savings generated

by lower absenteeism, lower health care costs, and improved performance. Also, 35 percent of employees with children under 15 would
move to new employers if they could have more flexibility.

The Employee Services Management magazine suggests these rea-
sons for offering family activities:

- It's easier to get employees to come outside work hours if they
  know they can bring the family.
- Employees that learn more about each other and share more expe-
  riences trust each other more and work better together.
- Family activities create more goodwill for your company.
- Having a company-planned event relieves stress on the employee
  who usually has to schedule and plan everything. Ready-made pro-
  grams save employees planning time, too!
- They keep employees focused on the job, not making plans.
- Group activities keep costs down. This saves money.
- Your events may be the only time children are exposed to a par-
  ticular activity.
- Your programs help employees and their families create memories.[8]

Support family-friendly programs and policies. These are just some
of the programs organizations have instituted to help their employees
blend work and family:

- Flextime
- Job sharing
- Telecommuting
- Part-time career paths
- Early retirement
- Relocation services

- Job placement services for spouses
- Childcare
- Eldercare
- Family Medical Leave Act
- Paternity/Maternity leave
- Adoption programs
- Employee Assistance Programs
- Legal assistance programs
- Financial assistance programs
- Employee-assisted housing
- Tuition reimbursement programs
- Scholarship programs
- Employee training on life issues
- Sabbaticals
- "Choice" time
- Payroll deduction programs
- Forgivable loans, repayable loans, grants, and interest-rate buy-down
- On-site medical care
- Education/Hobby classes
- Concierge services
- Wellness programs
- Corporate errand runner
- Exercise equipment or fitness center
- Full-time handyman
- On-site chaplains
- Bible study, meditation classes, and support/prayer groups
- Opportunities for community service

In planning a long-term strategy for organizational support of work/home initiatives, keep in mind the Life-cycle Approach that is prevalent in our culture today: New Hire, Marriage/Partner, Children, Divorce, Blended Family, College, Eldercare, Retirement. Each stage has its own unique needs. Consider in what stages your employees are functioning and then prioritize the needs for programs and services.

Here are some other ways to involve families[9]:

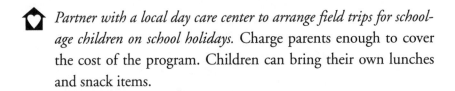

Partner with a local day care center to arrange field trips for school-age children on school holidays. Charge parents enough to cover the cost of the program. Children can bring their own lunches and snack items.

Work with a local movie theater to arrange a movie showing on a Saturday morning for employees and their families. Because the theater is not used at that time management will probably charge little or nothing for rental. You might even get the movie at the local library to save on expenses.

Hold a bike rodeo. Use the services of nonprofit agencies like the police department to oversee bike safety.

Have a Kids' Clothes Closet. Allow employees to use a room and tables and chairs to sell children's clothing, toys, furniture, and books to other employees. Volunteers can be recruited to help set up and price items.

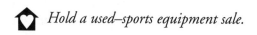 *Hold a used–sports equipment sale.*

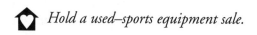 *Offer an Easter Egg Hunt.*

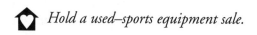 *Hold a Pasta Night for families.* Volunteers can cook the meal or work with your food-service program. To help defray costs, set up a cash bar for drinks. Door prizes make it more fun.

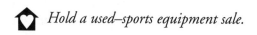 *Organize a bus trip to a destination about an hour away and invite families*—a shopping mall, amusement park, ball game, zoo, etc.

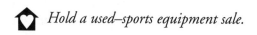 *Have camp buses pick up children at the worksite during vacations.*

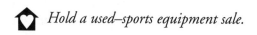 *Consider programs to help all ages of families.*

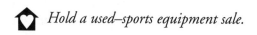 *Provide close-in parking for expectant mothers.*

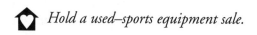 *Supply beepers for expectant fathers working away from telephones.*

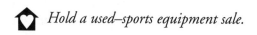 *Donate scholarships, money, volunteer efforts, fixtures, and supplies to childcare providers and agencies.* Other ways to help are to provide a resource center for family day care providers and offer assistance with recruiting and training childcare providers.

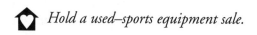 *Have car seats available to borrow.*

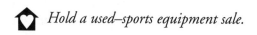 *Create summer jobs for college-age children of employees.*

♥ *Fund extended hours of nearby childcare and Saturday childcare hours when parents must work.*

♥ *Provide special programs for children on days when there is no school.* These could be as simple as showing Disney movies in the company auditorium.

♥ *Arrange discounts for necessities such as diapers, formula, and over-the-counter medications.*

♥ *Hold after-school seminars for latchkey kids.* Tap the great expertise in many different and interesting areas in your workforce. Encourage employees to sign up to share their talents, hobbies, and interests with other employees' children.

♥ *Launch a working parents newsletter.* Many publications will give permission to reprint articles of interest to parents. Be sure that this newsletter contains a bit of humor as well. It should be positive, uplifting, and helpful.

♥ *Set up a computer bulletin board information-exchange site for families.* There could be different "rooms" for various stages of family life.

♥ *Start eldercare counseling and hold seminars on aging.*

♥ *Create a work/family library on marriage, parenting, and aging.*

Help to organize a "Bring Your Family to Work" day or an Open House, Expo, or Fair in which families come to learn more about what their relatives do. Make sure that various activities are planned for different age groups, and always serve some kind of food to create an atmosphere of celebration. If your workforce population is diverse, be sure you staff booths with bilingual personnel.

Have a "Family Fun Day." Schedule a special day for families on a workday with games for adults and children. The objectives for family days at work are:

1. To bring parents and children together for a day of fun, filled with structured activities at the workplace
2. To teach children more about their parents' work (including what they do, where they work, who they work with, and how long it takes them to get to work)
3. To improve communication between parents and children about work
4. To reinforce for children the positive aspects of working

 The American Hospital Association sponsored a *"Day for Play at Work"* at their Chicago headquarters. Activities included making a "memory button" of the day, creating a family album of "what kind of work each member of the family does," having a Polaroid family portrait taken in the work environment, and playing with computers, phones, and other office equipment. The organization provided refreshments, balloons, Frisbees, and other party favors, and a take-home booklet for parents and children to work on together. In the afternoon the parents took their children on a boat ride on Lake Michigan.

Create a Kids' Day. The human resources staff at CanWest Gas Supply, Inc., in Vancouver, British Columbia, decided to implement a program for employees' children to spend a day at the office. During their summer vacation or a school break, children of CanWest employees can visit their parents' office for a day to see what they do and find out how an office really runs. The program boosts morale, helps develop camaraderie among departments, introduces some humor and fun into the workplace, and helps children better understand their parents' activities away from home. Bruna Martinuzzi, the manager of administration and human resources, explains the day:

We send each child a letter inviting him or her to spend Kids' Day at CanWest. We stress punctuality to (help the child) develop good habits. The child's day starts at 8 AM. When the child arrives, Jackie, the payroll and pension clerk, greets him or her. Jackie and the parent bring the child to my office. The child then meets a few people and takes part in about half an hour of welcome activities. From 8:30 to 9 we give the child a lecture on what natural gas is and what the company does, what Mom or Dad does, and how she or he fits into the organization. We give the child several brochures on natural gas that he or she can take home.

From 9:30 to 10 the child learns about our e-mail system. We put the child on e-mail for the day so his or her name appears in the system. Usually a friend or parent will send the child e-mail. From 10 to 10:15 Jackie and the child's parent take the child down to the cafeteria where they take a break. From 10:15 to 10:45 the child goes downstairs with the office coordinator and picks up the mail. Then they deliver the mail so the child gets to tour all the offices. From 10:45 to noon, it's time for hands-on computer training. We show the child the computer system that we use so he or she learns a little bit of word processing. Jackie helps the child create a little system for himself or herself such as budgeting an allowance. From 12 to 12:30 the child goes to lunch with his or her parent. Sometimes other employees join them.[10]

The afternoon is filled with similar activities that the children love, and parents line up to bring their children in!

There are many other creative ideas for family days at work

 Have a Children's Fishing Derby. This event has been offered to the members of the CIGNA Employees Activities Club in Hartford, Connecticut, since 1962. The campus includes a three-acre pond that is stocked with 100 bass the night before the derby, which is held in late May or early June. Trophies are given and each child receives trinket prizes and juice boxes during the event.[11]

 The Association of Compaq Employees (ACE) of Compaq Computer Corporation, Houston, Texas, *conducts a Fall Festival* for Compaq employees and their families in October, which is centered around the Halloween theme. Components of the festival include carnival rides and games, food concessions, and a haunted house. The event is planned and conducted almost entirely by ACE volunteers.[12]

Kodak partners with the YMCA of Greater Rochester to offer *Holiday Week Fun Clubs and Summer Day Camp programs* for Rochester Kodak employees. These camps were started to help employees find quality care for their children during summer vacation and school week breaks. The camps are available to employees' children age 5 to 14 years old and provide an environment that develops friendships and strengthens self-esteem. These fun clubs are staffed by experienced YMCA camp counselors and provide convenient work-site drop-off and pickup locations. Local sponsors also support Science and Technology Summer Camps that are designed and operated by the 4-H Youth Development Program of Cornell Cooperative Extension. Eight one-week sessions focus on weekly themes: space, water, architecture, plants, animals, nutrition, insects, power, and more. Each day combines hands-on science education and discovery with fun summertime recreation, including swimming.[13]

 Miller Brewing Company's employee association at the corporate offices in Milwaukee, Wisconsin, holds a *winter event* that can be adapted for any climate. Planned by a committee of employees, MACfest is a full-day Saturday event at an area resort. They negotiate a discounted hotel rate for Saturday night for employees and their families, and a dozen activities are on the agenda for the day.[14]

 You might also have a *Mother/Daughter day* at work or a *Father/Son day*, a *Parent/Child day*, an *Aunt/Uncle/Child day*, or a *Grandparent/Grandchild day*. Another addition might be an "Adopt a Daughter or Son" day.

Day-care guilt.

Get everyone involved. CUNA Mutual Mortgage Company sponsored a work/family day and asked everyone to help:

> *You'll be showing your workstation to your family, so we thought some simple decorative touches for your department might be nice. ALL employees are invited to:*
> - *Create a simple, colorful WELCOME banner for your area or float some festive balloons.*
> - *If simple visuals or other types of work demonstrations would help your family understand your work, set them up.*

- *Create a photograph board of all department members so your family can finally see what coworker "Bill" looks like.*
- *Come up with your own ideas to make your area special and attractive for your family.*

Decorate your workplace in ways that celebrate families

St. Catherine Hospital in Garden City, Kansas, held a *door-decorating contest, "LOVE is . . ."* Employees brought pictures of their families and decorated around the pictures.

A senior HR person tells how her department uses bulletin boards: "Our department *prepared bulletin boards.* Each person did one with pictures of our family members. Now when people come to our office, they look at the wall with our bulletin boards and they learn something about us before they come to see us. These bulletin boards reflect us as human beings."

At Ingalls Memorial Hospital in Harvey, Illinois, Joyce Lewis, Lab Supervisor, started a *photo gallery* draped in red, white, and blue bunting to honor the loved ones of laboratory employees who are serving in the armed forces. Not only is this a source of pride for the department, but it is also a comfort for the employees whose relatives are far away.[15]

Offer *Work-Life Retreats* for your employees. These retreats are organized weekends (or several days) away from the work site that bring families together to improve skills and develop support systems to find a better balance in their lives. The content is based on the issues that employees and their families want to address. Some of the options are:

- *Whole life planning*
- *Skills and role-plays* in conflict resolution
- *Skills for communicating* more effectively with spouses/significant others, children, elders, and others in their lives
- *Strategies for organizing time* for self, spouse, family members, and friends
- *Strategies for dealing with guilt*
- *Ways of developing a Family Mission*
- *Ways of staying healthy*
- *Developing support systems*

Recent studies at Fel-Pro, Inc., and Johnson & Johnson have shown that work-life programs can positively impact morale, retention, and quality of work. Feeling supported by the organization and armed with new skills and strategies empowers employees and positively affects their attitudes and commitment to work. When workers feel in control of their personal lives and they're working with their partners to create a better balance, these factors will affect their worklives in a positive way, so Work-Life Retreats are good news for both employers and employees.

Start special recognition for spouses and families. John Farrell, senior director for Carlson Marketing Group (CMG), a Minneapolis-based relationship marketing company, says, "Awards must inspire increased performance, must engage the family, and must change behavior." Any time an organization recognizes the sacrifice and contributions of the employee's family, they are helping create a feeling of teamwork, both within the family and with the organization itself. When family members feel included, appreciated, and a part of the mission of the company, they are much more willing to support the employee in his or her work. This not only helps build loyalty to the company, but it also increases productivity by reducing strife at home.

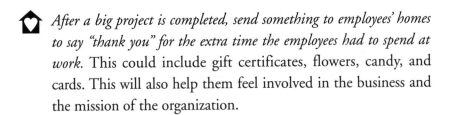 *After a big project is completed, send something to employees' homes to say "thank you" for the extra time the employees had to spend at work.* This could include gift certificates, flowers, candy, and cards. This will also help them feel involved in the business and the mission of the organization.

The Four Seasons Hotel near Puerto Vallarta, Mexico, *honors two families each month* by providing a special lunch in the employee dining room and a tour of the facility. When the family is included and acknowledged, a sense of pride and mutual respect usually follows.

Send a gift to an employee's family for Thanksgiving or Christmas. A number of my clients have sent copies of my book *CARE Packages for the Home—Dozens of Ways to Regenerate Spirit Where You Live* to all their employees' homes as a Christmas or Thanksgiving gift, along with a letter of appreciation from the CEO or another senior person. This supports the Baxter Labs global study in which the one thing employees most wanted was "to be respected as whole human beings with a life outside of work." The book contains ideas for single people, single parents, blended families, extended families, grandparents, and retirees as well as traditional families.

 Honor employees' spouses and partners. Travis White, CEO of Centillium Technology, decided to build loyalty and avert high turnover by involving the family. He invited employees' spouses and partners, the ones who suffer most from the overtime work of their significant others, especially in a start-up company, to a Saturday party. He told the employees themselves to stay home and take care of the kids! After a short talk about the business, he surprised each of the partners with 250 shares of Centillium stock. This delightful strategy gave the spouses a definite stake in the work their partners are doing as well as honoring their support and commitment to their significant others.

Recognize children and spouse accomplishments. Start an "I'm Proud" bulletin board for employees to post accomplishments of their families.

Use employees' families and children in your ads. Instead of hiring models, use your own employees and their families to advertise your products or services. This not only promotes authenticity, but it also builds employee buy-in and loyalty.

Call their mothers. I have recently been sharing a very creative appreciation idea with all my audiences. Two years ago after I had spoken to a large manufacturing firm, one of the managers stayed to talk with me. He said, "Barbara, I have the lowest performing team in the whole company. Never once have they ever met their goals. But you got me thinking. I'm going to call and tell you what happens."

Almost nine months later, I received a call from this man. He was ecstatic! He said, "After you were there, I got the whole team together, and I said to them, 'OK. For any of you who reach your goal this quarter, I'm going to call your mother!'"

He said for the first time ever, *single people on his team met their goals!* And he said the calls were one of the nicest things he ever did. Some of the mothers cried, and others were simply delighted. I don't care how old we are, if someone thanks our family for the great job we are doing, it feels wonderful. And all it cost was a few phone calls!

I recently received this e-mail from Jim Gwinn, Chairperson of the Christian Management Association (CMA) Board:

> *I am so thankful for the message you gave at CMA on expressing care and love for others. Have used the "Call their Moms or wives to say thanks" idea a few times. It is unbelievable what an impact that has on Moms and then on the persons. All the employees I have done this for have called me in tears, saying, "No one has ever thanked my Mom for my life in that manner." THANK YOU for such an insightful thought. Only wish I had called your husband and told him what a treasure you are and thank him for sharing you with us.*

Whose mother, spouse, or significant other might you call today to show your appreciation for that person?

Include some of the following ideas to involve families

 Purchase company memberships at local attractions such as zoos, museums, amusement parks, and sports arenas. Then make these memberships available to employees' families. This not only saves them money, but it also encourages families to spend more time together.

Invite employees' families to excess goods sales. When you have leftover products, give employees' family members first choice to purchase them. This will be a perk for them and will allow them to enjoy the products their relatives help create.

Hold weekend and evening personal computer classes for families. This becomes a way to further educate and develop your employees while at the same time providing a family experience that they will appreciate. The family that learns together will be closer in many ways.

Hold open workshops on drug and alcohol abuse for the entire family.

Set aside a small room for nursing mothers who return to the workplace. This gives them a clean, comfortable place to express their milk and store it under refrigeration.

Start contests at your workplace that involve families

The Department of Motor Vehicles in Virginia sponsored a wonderful contest in which *they asked family members to draw pictures of what their Mom/Dad/Grandpa/Grandma/Aunt/Uncle did at work all day.* The pictures were so delightful that they framed them, and their hallways and reception areas now are filled with the children's drawings. Not only do their customers enjoy them and the atmosphere they create, but the children love to come in and see THEIR drawings hanging where their family members work!

Provide concierge services for employees. Making life easier can be more valuable to people than getting extra cash. Employee Assistance Programs now exist that offer concierge services such as *grocery shopping, dry cleaning, laundry, "meals-to-go,"* and *household repairs and maintenance.* By getting help accomplishing mundane household chores at work, employees can spend time away from the office in a more relaxing, enjoyable manner—which translates into a happier, more loyal workforce.

 A story in the *Success in Recruiting and Retaining* newsletter tells about Wilton Connor Packaging of Charlotte, North Carolina. They found that most of the employees did not own washers and dryers and had to take public transportation to laundromats, so this is what they did:

The company started a full-service laundry benefit *for its 500 workers that let them drop off their wash in the morning and pick it up at the end of the workday. The cost to the company and its workers is paltry: Workers pay $1 a basket and a quarter for each pressed item of clothing, and the company chips in an equal amount. Costs are kept low by guaranteeing the laundry service regular business. Wendy Walker, the firm's human resources manager, says the perk is "the most popular thing among our employees." Along with two other creative perks tied to its specific workforce—a staff handyman to help employees with minor*

*home repairs and tutors for employees with school-age children—the
laundry perk has helped to keep the firm's turnover at next to nothing—
1 percent a year. Walker told* Human Resource Executive, *"People
know that this is a fair company and a good company to work for
because we are sensitive to our employees' everyday needs."*[16]

 Datex-Ohmeda, a Tewksbury, Massachusetts–based anesthesia
and critical care company, realized that the incentive their employees appreciated most was the gift of time. As a result *they signed up
with Boston-based corporate concierge Circles.* Now all 1,700 North
American workers and their spouses can call or send an e-mail
request for help. Employees can make unlimited requests for such
things as dental appointments, household help, hard-to-get tickets, or weekend getaways, and these requests are filled in a couple
of days. The company personalizes its rewards while keeping its
cash outlay manageable. The benefits manager estimates that
because employees' nagging concerns are soothed, the firm saved
280 work hours in the first quarter alone. They also provide a dry
cleaner and a *mobile on-site car wash and detailing operation.*[17]

 According to a December 2000 article in the *Success in Recruiting and Retaining* newsletter, Julie Ferrier at OneSoft in McLean,
Virginia, acts as the *company "Mom"* to help make employees' lives
better. She arranges for dry-cleaning pickup, provides an iron and
ironing board and sewing kits, sells stamps and even addresses
wedding invitations. She says, "Employees can go anywhere and
get any amount of money, but I think it's the little perks that keep
people."[18]

A number of large companies have hired a full-time concierge *or corporate errand runner* to help busy employees with personal business. They make restaurant reservations, purchase tickets, buy gifts for special occasions, hire baby-sitters, track down recipes, and plan anniversary getaways. Lack of time for personal business has become a major employee gripe in many companies today, and many organizations feel that having a concierge available has improved morale and lowered stress in significant ways.

Here are some other creative ideas to help employees with time issues:

- Bill payment center
- Video drop box
- On-site photofinishing
- Prescription service
- Sell stamps
- Sell bus tokens
- Aerobics classes
- Nutrition seminars
- On-site flu shots
- Self-defense classes

- Smoking cessation programs
- Weight Watchers classes
- Toastmasters classes
- Walking program
- On-site chair massages
- Cancer prevention programs
- Book discussion groups
- Parenting classes
- Shared vacation time

Ensure that employees have flexible hours. This perk is the one most requested by employees today, according to all the current research. Linda Saikas, an Interim Training Officer in the Small Business Development Centers of Ohio, expressed it this way: "I am fortunate to have flexible hours. This is a tremendous benefit if you have a medical appointment or late school start time, or if you want to take a shorter lunch and finish the workday earlier." A Chicago bank's employees can ask their managers for flexible schedules to allow for doctor visits, school conferences, and other needs. They have had cases where employees have chosen them over another employer because of the more flexible schedule. The National Futures Association started a policy allowing workers to arrange flexible schedules with their managers as long as they work 75 hours every two weeks. Allowing employees some flexibility in their schedules helps them live more comfortably and with less stress as they try to manage the other responsibilities in their lives.

Create a corporate culture that respects and values families and shows trust for employees. The mere existence of work-life programs does not guarantee the elimination of high employee stress and low morale. Managers play a critical role in developing a corporate culture that makes work-life balance programs acceptable. The culture must support the programs. Think about what behaviors are valued and rewarded. For example, are meetings routinely called at 7 AM or at 6 PM— or on weekends? Are vacations interrupted at the behest of anxious customers? Is it OK to take off in the middle of the day to help out at your child's school? Do you have to cancel training events at the last minute because managers say they are too busy?

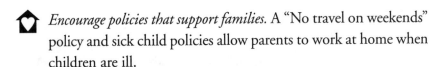 *Encourage policies that support families.* A "No travel on weekends" policy and sick child policies allow parents to work at home when children are ill.

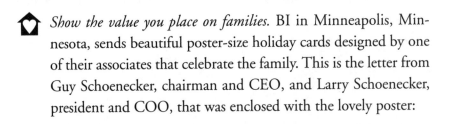 *Show the value you place on families.* BI in Minneapolis, Minnesota, sends beautiful poster-size holiday cards designed by one of their associates that celebrate the family. This is the letter from Guy Schoenecker, chairman and CEO, and Larry Schoenecker, president and COO, that was enclosed with the lovely poster:

The combination of love and family provides a powerful foundation for our united efforts to make a better world. Our children learn by watching us, as we learned from our parents. We know you take your role as a teacher very seriously, and we encourage you to find the joy in exploring your children's possibilities every day.

The holidays present us with the opportunity to review our personal beliefs and values. At BI, we remain committed to faith, family, and friends.

Since 1975, we have proudly sent our friends, associates, and customers an original holiday poster greeting. These "limited edition" prints are created by BI associates to share with you. We display them in our lobby, and are pleased to say that many of you cherish them in your home.

Enjoy your family time, especially during the holiday season. Thank you for your business and your friendship. Best wishes to you and yours throughout the New Year.

It is obvious that the company values the family!

When appropriate, offer suggestions and information. This data could include a backup directory for childcare and eldercare; a way to set up an informal system for ensuring children check-in after school; lists of resources on childcare and eldercare, and workshops to improve home-time management, communication, and dealing with guilt; alternative work schedules; and family counseling during a relocation. It is interesting to note that according to a family historian at Evergreen State College in Olympia, Washington, one out of every four households is giving substantial time and assistance to an aging parent, so help with caretaking is not just an issue for employees with children!

Recruit families. Dell Computer Corporation in Austin, Texas, doesn't just recruit candidates; it also recruits their families because relocating affects everyone. Many times the decision to come to Dell is based on matters completely unrelated to work such as finding the right job for a spouse, finding the right school, house, doctor, or church. They routinely spend time talking to the spouses of recruits to match up their family needs with resources in the area—to do whatever it takes to communicate to recruits the virtues of life outside Dell and the importance of the whole family being happy rather than just the benefits of working at the company.

Honor the needs of single employees. As you consider using some of these ideas to blend work and family in your organization, it is critically important to honor the needs of single employees, too. In a powerful article by Carol Kleiman in the *Chicago Tribune* titled "Family-friendly benefits snub singles," the writer points out that many single people feel left out of company-sponsored family-friendly programs and feel put upon by colleagues with families. They seem to always be asked to work holidays or overtime and when they occasionally ask to take unscheduled time off, permission is often denied. According to Thomas Coleman, an attorney and executive director of the American Association for Single People, some 40 percent of the workforce is unmarried and 60 percent of the workforce doesn't have a child under the age of 18 in the household. Organizations must respect the needs of ALL employees, single or married, for everyone needs a life outside of work to renew himself or herself. Some answers Kleiman suggests may include more open communication, asking employees to be honest about what their individual needs and desires are, and cafeteria-based benefits plans.[19]

An article in *HR Magazine* titled "The Baby Blues" quotes Rita, a childless 30-something graphic artist in New York, who believes that she is being cheated by today's family-friendly workplace. Over and over she has stayed late when her coworkers skipped out to pick up their kids at day care or left to attend their children's soccer games. "Today, companies aren't family-friendly, they're family-focused—to the point that people like me, who don't have children, are completely excluded from the conversation."[20]

Elinor Burkett, the author of *The Baby Boon: How Family-Friendly America Cheats the Childless,* says that the resentment is fueled by the perception that the majority of the workforce, those without young children, must cover for the minority, those with young children. One remedy is to offer cash back to employees without children as a rebate on health benefits and childcare subsidies. Another option is to add more benefits that appeal to all employees such as offering convenience services like dry cleaning and gourmet take-out dinners. Another help would be for human resources to offer personal floating days or general leaves of absence that aren't tied to specific criteria. Even changing the name of your program from "work/family" to "work/life" will help to balance out everyone's needs. According to the U.S. Bureau of Census Population Division, "The most common type of household after 2005 will be comprised of single persons and married couples without children."

PUTTING IT ALL TOGETHER

An article by Charles Fishman titled "Moving Toward a Balanced Life" in *Workforce* magazine shares how SAS Institute, Inc., in Raleigh, North Carolina, incorporates all the principles of work-life balance. "SAS Institute isn't an employer—it's a provider. Employees don't have to worry about balancing work and life because they're one and the same." They have the capacity for childcare for 700 preschool children, and the cost is low. "They have free access to a 36,000-square-foot gym, a putting green, sky-lit meditation rooms, and the services of a full-time in-house eldercare consultant. There's a pianist in the café at lunchtime and all the free juice and soda employees want. Every white-collar employee has a private office and the opportunity to create a flexible work schedule, and for everyone, the standard workweek is 35 hours." Paid vacation for all employees is three weeks plus the week off that SAS gives everyone from Christmas to New Year's, and after ten years of service, a fourth week (really fifth) is added.

All staff, no matter what the position, receive the same benefits that include:

- Three subsidized cafeterias
- Casual dress every day
- Profit sharing
- Domestic-partner benefits
- No limit to sick days
- Free health insurance
- An on-site medical clinic staffed by doctors and nurse practitioners
- Free laundering of gym clothes, with return the next morning to your locker
- Soccer fields, baseball diamonds, coed workout areas, and single-sex workout areas, pool tables

When a new benefit is suggested, there is a process for approving it:

- Does the benefit fit the culture at SAS?
- Would it have a positive effect on a significant number of employees and their families?
- Is it cost-accountable—would the benefit be valued by those using it at the same level as the expense of providing it?

This company has created a culture of loyalty, and, as a result, they have one of the lowest turnover rates in the software world, never more than 5 percent a year. Not only is treating people well the right thing to do, according to Jim Goodnight, SAS's CEO and founder, but it is also profitable. The *Harvard Business Review* recently calculated that SAS's low turnover saves the company $75 million a year, enough to spend $12,000 extra a year on benefits for each employee.

David Russo, the former director of human resources, says: "This is not the 'good ship Lollipop.' The benefits we offer are just the tangible stuff that represent [founder] Jim Goodnight's philosophy. A lot of companies think they have created a culture of caring, but the employees don't feel it. People put things together, but they are counter to the culture, and they are not being used. Jim's idea is, if you hire adults and treat them like adults, they'll behave like adults."[21]

While your organization may not be able to offer all these benefits, I would encourage you to ask your employees what they would like and then devise a five-year plan. Start with easy, low-cost things—always working toward a culture that truly values its people.

This was a powerful letter to the editor in *Fast Company* magazine:

Your magazine does a wonderful job of capturing the excitement, creativity, and profit potential of the entrepreneurial life. For many of your readers, the gratifications of this life can easily surpass those of family and community.

May I offer your readers one word of caution? As they read about extraordinary customer service, home phone numbers on business cards, and 80-hour workweeks, they might want to reflect on their own childhood experiences with the proverbial "absent father in the gray flannel suit."

History has a wonderful way of repeating itself. It wouldn't do your readers any harm, as they're turning the pages of this fine magazine, to reflect on the "customers" closer to home. Those customers, after all, will become their core "team" the day after they receive the gold watch.[22]

Baird K. Brightman, Ph.D., President Worklife Strategies, Sudbury, Massachusetts (www.wklf.com)

4

Blending Work and Friends

Friends are family we choose for ourselves.

Sharon Mills

A RECENT *Industry Week* survey and the *International Workplace Values Survey*, which involved 1,200 people in 18 countries, suggests that people in business experience a deep sense of isolation, and more than two thirds of them expressed an interest in feeling a greater sense of belonging in the workplace.[1] Susan Michie and Anne Cockroft of London's Royal Free Hospital and School of Medicine, writing in the *British Medical Journal,* conclude that "increased pace of work over the preceding five years and a *lack of social contact with colleagues* during spare time were . . . associated with an increased risk of myocardial infarction [heart attack]." More fatal heart attacks occur at 9 AM Monday than at any other time.[2]

Barbara Moses, the author of *Career Intelligence: The 12 New Rules for Work and Life Success,* relates how people confess their most significant relationships are suffering:

When asked how they would like to spend their time outside work, they say, "Forget spending time with friends—just spending time with my children is a luxury."[3]

> **To have a friend is one of the sweetest gifts that life can bring; to be a friend is to have a solemn and tender education of the soul from day to day.**
>
> Amy Robertson Brown

This is all the more reason to encourage friendships during the workday.

Other current research shows that if an employee has a good friend at work, he or she is less likely to leave. Because the average cost today to replace an employee is $50,000, organizations should do everything possible to keep employees happy. One of the easiest ways to do this is to encourage relationships that go beyond the world of work.

INDIVIDUAL IDEAS

Share your work with friends outside of the job. This will help you develop an even deeper relationship with them when they see you in your workplace and better understand that facet of your life.

 Invite a friend to your workplace for lunch once a month. When building relationships, it is important for friends to see us in our

**Stella knew the importance of being discreet
when making personal phone calls.**

work environment. Besides, you have to have lunch anyway, so why not make it even more enjoyable by planning to spend time with someone you like and perhaps do not get to see often?

 Invite a friend to go on a business trip with you. If your hotel room is already being paid, your friend will only have the costs of airfare and meals to absorb, and usually the client will plan some fun things for you to do.

Give your friends your business cards and ask them to network for you if it is appropriate. Then you reciprocate.

Work on developing new friendships with coworkers

Each week invite one person in your organization you would like to get to know better to lunch. You will make new friends at work during a time you are there anyway. If finances are a problem, bring a lunch for them.

Plan an outside activity with coworkers. Go hiking, enjoy a picnic, or take up bowling. You might even include family members.

Start a "Dinner Club" with coworkers who become friends. You can implement this idea whether you are single, single with children, married without children, or married with children. If you do have children, here is a strategy to help with childcare. Each parent or set of parents can take turns hosting all the children for dinner once a month. (It is even better if the children are involved—in setting the table, serving, food planning and preparation, cleanup, dinner-table games, etc.) This gives the other parents a night off and encourages deeper workplace relationships both with the parents and with their children.

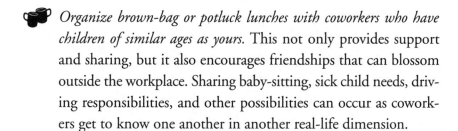

Organize brown-bag or potluck lunches with coworkers who have children of similar ages as yours. This not only provides support and sharing, but it also encourages friendships that can blossom outside the workplace. Sharing baby-sitting, sick child needs, driving responsibilities, and other possibilities can occur as coworkers get to know one another in another real-life dimension.

One day a week meet with coworkers for a racquetball game or a pizza. When you do something on a regular basis, relationships develop quickly.

Plan to meet for breakfast twice a month with a new friend at work.

Personalize relationships with coworkers. Sit down with the people you work with and ask them about themselves. Everyone has a story! People want to be cared for and possess a sense of their personal growth and value. As we create more meaningful relationships at work, we are enriching our own lives.

Here are some fun conversation starters:

1. If you could invite four famous people from history over for dinner, who would they be?
2. If you could possess one superpower, which would you choose and why: to fly, to be invisibile, to have X-ray vision, or to read minds?
3. If you were given $10,000 and you could not save or invest it, what would you do with the money?

4. If you could travel back in time, where *would you go* and when?
5. If you were going away for a year and could bring only three of your possessions, what would they be?
6. If you had the power to enact one new law, what would it be?
7. List 20 things that make you happy. Then share your lists. This gives you wonderful opportunities to make the other person happy.

Plan a holiday gathering. In November invite fellow workers to your home. Ask each person to bring a craft or a food to share for the holidays.

 Krista Kurth and Suzanne Adele Schmidt, authors of *Running on Plenty at Work,* share how one of their seminar participants encourages interacting at work:

A person who loves to play chess at home puts a magnetic chessboard on his office door with a sign inviting people to make a move using the white pieces. He checks the board periodically throughout the day, sees what move has been made, and makes a move himself. This activity doesn't take much of his time during the day and gives him a fun way to interact with people at work. He takes a short break and uses his mind in a way that is renewing for him.[4]

 Invite both a personal friend or neighbor and a coworker to lunch. This is a wonderful way to share your friends with others at work and to create a larger network of those who are important in your life.

Share emergency childcare with a coworker. Find a coworker with similar values and parenting style as well as children close to the same ages as yours. When one of you has a sick child and cannot miss work, share the responsibility of childcare by alternating which person stays home with the child. You may also work together to share a caretaker, such as a grandparent or a spouse, when emergencies arise.

> The bond that links your true family is not one of blood, but of respect and joy in each other's life.
>
> Richard Bach

Share tasks with a coworker-friend. One way to be happier at work as well as enjoy a friendship is to share certain tasks. Find out what your friend really likes to do that perhaps you don't enjoy so much and trade the work. Perhaps one of you loves to organize and file and the other would much rather conduct research on the Internet.

Not only is it wonderfully helpful to have someone do the chores you dislike, but it is also fun to have a buddy with whom to share!

Create your own "dream team." A "dream team," according to Fire "Captain Bob," consists of spouses, partners, friends, coworkers, relatives, employees, customers, and vendors. These dream team members are there to support you and make your life easier. You may have different team members for the specific areas of your life: work, family, friends, health, spirit, and service.

Get to know someone new each week or month. Dan Bent of Honolulu, Hawaii, made it a point to call someone he didn't know in his Rotary Club, a national organization for businesspeople, and ask him if he would like a ride to the luncheon meeting. These drives, which could be up to 25 minutes long, changed many relationships in the group of 380 members. Not only was Dan eventually asked to be the president of the group, but, more important, he feels a special bond with each of the persons he reached out to whenever he sees them. These relationships have been important in both his personal and his professional lives.

Start a support group of friends in your same work circumstances.
Bill Higgins, who is married to New York real estate impresario Barbara
Corcoran, founded Spouseclub, an informal network of men with
powerful, career-oriented wives. This group was formed to promote
camaraderie and sharing and even has an
informal Web site, <www.spouseclub.com>,
for making contacts and swapping ideas.
Spouses Trailing Under Duress (STUDS)
is a Brussels-based organization made up
of men who have relocated because of their
wives' careers. They host weekly luncheons,
cycling trips, sightseeing, children's play
groups, and golf outings.

> **Our job is not to straighten each other out, but to help each other up.**
>
> Neva Coyle

ORGANIZATIONAL IDEAS

Encourage communities in the workplace. One of the ways we can
stay connected and blend work and friends is to establish different kinds
of communities in the workplace.

Communities at work can be social, professional, spiritual, or political.
They can be based on special interests such as recreational pursuits, cultural and artistic interests, religious beliefs, or political causes. You may
even have a community of work friends whom you have never met but with
whom you interact through e-mail, telephone, and other electronic means.

Research shows that the more connections you have to various communities at work, the more likely you are to be satisfied with your job
and the more balanced you feel because there is less of a need for friends
outside of work.

According to an article in *Employee Services Management* magazine by Catrina Cerny, Gates Rubber Company, which has sites in many other countries, has founded a *Travel Club*. One feature of this club is a type of exchange program in which the employee services department acts as an intermediary for traveling workers. Through the club, a worker from the United States can visit another country and save accommodation dollars, and can also meet people from this culture on a more personal basis. Then the favor is returned at a later time by the American worker. What a wonderful way to build global relationships within your organization![5]

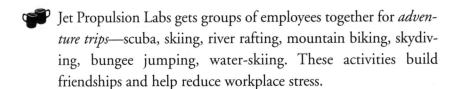 Jet Propulsion Labs gets groups of employees together for *adventure trips*—scuba, skiing, river rafting, mountain biking, skydiving, bungee jumping, water-skiing. These activities build friendships and help reduce workplace stress.

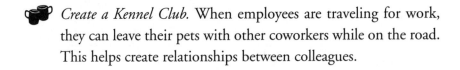 *Create a Kennel Club.* When employees are traveling for work, they can leave their pets with other coworkers while on the road. This helps create relationships between colleagues.

Help to create support groups in the workplace

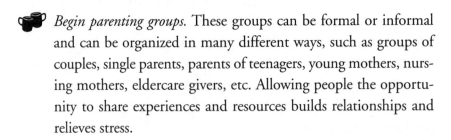 *Begin parenting groups.* These groups can be formal or informal and can be organized in many different ways, such as groups of couples, single parents, parents of teenagers, young mothers, nursing mothers, eldercare givers, etc. Allowing people the opportunity to share experiences and resources builds relationships and relieves stress.

Organize reading groups. These may be based on the type of books read—novels, biographies, parenting books, etc.—or they may simply be discussion groups to get people started reading like the book group at Dearborn Trade Publishing in Chicago, Illinois (the publisher of this book), has organized.

 Encourage specialty support groups. Support small groups, either formal or informal, for those who have gone through a divorce, those who have lost a spouse, or those who have lost a child. Other specialty support groups may be for losing weight, quitting smoking, or even supporting marriages.

As a part of encouraging friendships in the workplace, it is important to open up avenues for employees to relate to one another as unique and special human beings. In the July/August 2002 issue of *Mosaics,* a publication by the Society for Human Resource Management, the focus was on workplace diversity. These are some of their suggestions for creating more understanding and tolerance, which can then lead to more sharing relationships and friendships in the workplace:

> **Friends are angels who lift us to our feet when our wings have trouble remembering how to fly.**

- *Sponsor an ethnic potluck luncheon.*
- *Hold a "brown-bag lunch" series to talk about diverse social and cultural issues.*
- *Create a display area where employees can post notices of events and activities happening in their communities.*

- *Provide employees with opportunities to attend local cultural events and exhibits.*
- *Start a mentoring program that pairs employees of diverse backgrounds, such as different age groups, cultures, or levels within the company.*[6]

Sponsor fun events that bring employees together

One organization had a bowling tournament between the departments in human resources—HR versus Training, HR versus Recruiting, etc. This not only promoted fun but created team building and bonding within the entire human resources department.

Many companies do fun things during the holidays such as organize "Secret Santas" or "Secret Pals"—activities in which each employee draws the name of another coworker and gives him or her small surprise gifts for a period of time. The special thing about an activity like this is that employees are focusing on the *personal* aspects of someone's life—what he or she values and desires. These delightful types of functions can take place at any time of the year. Sometimes they are more fun and less stressful when no holiday is involved.

Celebrate birthdays. It is vitally important to acknowledge employees' birthdays in some way. After all, it is the only day that is uniquely THEIRS. You may have a birthday cake or fill their workspace with balloons or send them a card personally signed by

the company president, but do not forget to honor them in some way. It is even more important not to forget the support staff. One of my favorite stories is about a night custodial person in a small company who was going to have a birthday. That day everyone emptied their own wastebaskets and in the bottom of each left a large circular handwritten note that said "Happy Birthday, _____." When the custodial person went around to empty the wastebaskets in the middle of the night, he was quite pleasantly surprised. Not only was he thrilled to receive the recognition and also relieved of one of his big chores, but the other employees found out how difficult his job really was!

> The bond that binds your true family is not one of blood, but of respect and joy in each other's life.
>
> Richard Bach

5

Blending Work and Health

Promoting the health of the "whole" person in the workplace is taking on a new meaning. Reduced productivity is a serious consequence of employee stress. Managers estimate that each employee who suffers from stress, anxiety, or depression loses 16 days of work per year.

Ruth Gordon Howard, RN, M.A., "A Fit Body and Fit Mind,"
Employee Services Management, January 1998

ALL NEW RESEARCH confirms that people who exercise at least 30 minutes three times a week are healthier and live longer. Because we spend more than half our lives at work, it seems wise to find creative ways to blend that exercise into our working day. Then, we are freed up to be truly available at home the rest of our day. It is also important to remember to take care of ourselves, for only then can we take care of the others in our lives.

INDIVIDUAL IDEAS

Find creative ways to exercise at work. Everything we read these days stresses the importance of exercise in our lives. Because we must spend at least eight hours of our day at work, why not find ways to get physical exercise during those hours to free up hours we can spend with our families in the evenings.

- *Work out during the lunch hour.* You might even choose one colleague to exercise with at least three times a week. This blends work, health, AND friends!

- Depending on your work situation, *walk with a friend, a child, or a coworker for part of each lunch hour.* Walking during half your lunch hour with a friend or colleague is an easy way to maintain fitness as well as catch up on his or her life. If you are like my friends and me, your mouth will get as much exercise as your legs!

- *Walk or run on a treadmill or ride an exercise bike while reading work-related materials.* This will also work if you have work-related videos to watch. Any time you can accomplish some work while you are also improving your health, you deserve accolades!

- *Bring your bike to work with you.* When Bonnie Michaels, the founder of Managing Work and Family, couldn't find a place to exercise when she was working at Keebler, she discovered she could take her bike in the car and then she could ride at lunch!

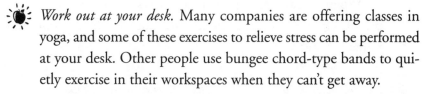
Work out at your desk. Many companies are offering classes in yoga, and some of these exercises to relieve stress can be performed at your desk. Other people use bungee chord-type bands to quietly exercise in their workspaces when they can't get away.

Start a walking club. Susan Dennett in Port St. Lucie, Florida, started a walking club where employees can log their miles. After they have walked 120 miles, the equivalent of walking to Disney World, they receive an award. She also started on-site yoga classes, which are sponsored by her company and are free to employees.

Find "Pockets of Peace." When stress is getting you down, find a place or discover a practice that brings you peace.

- *Take five-minute vacations.* When I am emotionally overdrawn, I take five-minute vacations that allow me some space to clear my mind. If I can, I go outside and walk around the building. If that is not possible, I go to the ladies' room, close the stall door, and visit the Bahamas for five minutes. You can do anything you want, and it doesn't even cost any money!

- *Listen to soothing music.* When you are stressed to the max, put your headphones on and listen for a few minutes to something that is soothing to you. I love the piano music of George Winston.

- *Call someone who loves you.* We all need to feel loved and valued, and that if we disappeared in the next hour, someone would miss us. When you are feeling down and stressed, call one of the people who thinks you are great and get a quick refill in your emotional bank account.

- *Do "the holes in the soles of your feet" exercise.* I love this exercise when I am stressed, and you can do it at your desk, in your car, or even in the boss's office! As you inhale deeply, think about breathing in all the love and goodness and light you can imagine. Then take all the stress, worry, and any other bad thoughts and imagine holes in the soles of your feet. As you exhale, push all those negative thoughts and feelings out through the holes in your feet. If you repeat this exercise five or six times, you certainly will feel much better!

Count your blessings. A favorite quotation of mine is from William Winter: "As much of Heaven is visible as we have eyes to see." When we look for good things, we can always find them, so open your eyes and look around you!

 Try prayer walking. Walking meditation is becoming the sport of choice for those people seeking to add meaning to their daily workout. Carolyn Scott Kortge, author of *The Spirited Walker: Fitness Walking for Clarity, Balance, and Spiritual Connection* and one of the top five ranked racewalkers in the United States, says, "There's a tremendous transformative power in prayer walking." She suggests you do two things in your prayer walking:

1. **Expect a miracle.** Set out in search of magic and look for things that capture your imagination.
2. **Walk in sacred places.** Wherever you walk, do so with the same reverence as if you were in a church or at a shrine.[1]

The wonderful thing about prayer **walking** is that it combines both health and spirit.

 Save an afternoon for a small treat just for you. Eat an ice-cream cone, walk in the park, or simply visit a quiet place where you can relax and gather your thoughts.

 Identify those things that are stressing you. Take a piece of paper and draw a line down the center. On the left side write down the stressors in your life that are inescapable. On the right side list stressors you can escape. Just seeing and knowing things you have no control over reduces stress. Then prioritize your escapable list and begin to ESCAPE!

 In their book *Running on Plenty at Work,* Krista Kurth and Suzanne Adele Schmidt share another idea to find peace in your workday:

A participant in one of our workshops shared that her preferred way to renew herself was to take a hot bath with nice smelling oils. Taking a bath at work was not an option, so we suggested that she think about how to modify this activity so that she could use it at work. She came up with a great idea. She decided to take a washcloth to work and create a hot, wet towel with aromatic oil on it, *like the towels you get at some restaurants or on some long airplane flights, by putting it in the micro- wave. Doing so allowed her to refresh herself at work by wiping her face and neck with the towel, breathing in the soothing aroma, and allowing the warmth to relax her neck.*[2]

> **He who has health has hope and he who has hope has everything.**
>
> An Arabian proverb

Begin healthy habits

 Set an alarm clock to go off every hour. Use that time to stretch and change your position. We get set in our habits and need reminders to keep us healthy.

 Bring healthy food for lunch and snacks. Keep a bag of oranges in the office refrigerator or in your desk. Then cut one into sections, keeping the peel on. It is easy and less messy to simply eat each section as you are working at your desk. Dried fruit is also a wonderful snack, and even popcorn is much healthier than candy or other salty snack foods. Bring sliced veggies and a low-fat dip, grape tomatoes, and granola bars as snacks.

 Forgo foods with caffeine, especially coffee.

 Drink lots of water. This not only keeps the toxins of stress flushed out of your system, but it provides valuable chemistry to keep your thinking alert and crisp. Add thin slices of lemon, orange, or lime. Some people even bring a special pitcher and glass to work with them. One of the ways I encourage myself to drink water is to keep a large plastic bottle with a plastic straw on my desk. During the day I try to refill it at least twice. It is amazing how unconsciously I drink the water when it is right there in front of me!

 Take the stairs. Instead of using the elevators during the day at work, take the stairs. Walk as much as you can. Park as far away from the building as possible each morning, and then get some good exercise as you walk to your office.

 Schedule a mammogram with a coworker once a year. Jill Bayer told me that she and her boss, the CFO, have an annual outing together—they schedule their yearly mammogram appointments at the same time and then they have lunch together. This practice combines work, health, and friends!

During an interview with *Working Woman* magazine, the Duchess of York was asked, *"Traveling so much, how do you manage to eat right on the road?"* She answered:

I'm gentle with myself. That's rule one. When I'm traveling, I don't beat myself up about not working out. My advice for working women who follow the same busy schedule I do is, first, just ease up on yourself a bit. Understand that you've achieved quite a lot in doing a good job and working hard. Second, drink more water—I'm up to five liters a day. Third, run and walk everywhere and avoid taking elevators. I run down hotel corridors because they're so long. But if you can't work out, wait until you get back. It's OK.[3]

Start a stress-free diet. Avoid foods that aggravate stress and choose those that improve your body's stores of the nutrients you need to handle stress.

Foods to Limit	Foods to Choose
Alcohol	Fresh fruits (especially citrus)
Coffee	Fresh vegetables
Chocolate	Herb teas
Cola drinks	Lean meat, fish, poultry
Tea	Whole grains
Sweets	Water
Junk food	Low-fat or nonfat dairy products
Refined flours	

Create a company cookbook of healthy recipes. This project is not only fun, but it also promotes healthy living, team building, and company loyalty.

ORGANIZATIONAL IDEAS

More than four in ten American workers (44 percent) are either very concerned or extremely concerned about stress from work demands, and 88 percent of them say the amount of stress they feel on the job is an important factor, according to a study conducted by economists at Rutgers University's John J. Heldrich Center for Workforce Development. The ability to balance work and family is the number one priority cited by those surveyed—more important than job security, quality of working environment, and relationships with coworkers and supervisors. About 87 percent of the workers reported they are concerned with getting enough sleep. It is vitally important that organizations today provide their employees ways to help reduce stress.[4]

Encourage exercise. All the research shows that exercise helps a person live longer, think better, and feel more alive. It only makes sense for employers to encourage and value physical activities if they want employees who are fit to do their best work.

 Provide workout rooms for employees. If employees can exercise easily before or after work or during breaks, they will be much more likely not to ignore this vitally important aspect of their health. The more convenient the organization can make it, the better, and EVERYONE will benefit! Some companies even provide same-sex workout places to honor the discomfort many feel in a coed setting. Bioware, the maker of video game Baldur's Gate, lets employees work out free at any city fitness center.

Provide equipment employees can use for various kinds of exercise. The Rockport Company in Marlborough, Massachusetts, *keeps a fleet of mountain bikes* for employees to burn off steam and calo-

"For cryin' out loud! Would you just take a sick day for once in your life!"

ries during lunchtime. Exercising during lunch reenergizes employees for a productive afternoon. The company is also planning to have a *reflexologist on-site* during specific times to administer foot massages to employees.

Help employees find places of peace and rest during their day at work

☀ *Provide pump rooms for nursing mothers.* Wells Fargo is one of 300 to 500 American companies with formal lactation programs. Their program provides new moms with a private space, a hospital-quality breast pump, a refrigerator where women can store bottles of milk, and a consultant who can answer questions. Some examples of positive results that organizations have experienced after adding such programs include:

- After the Los Angeles Department of Water & Power started its lactation program, nursing mothers began taking 27 percent fewer sick days to care for ill babies and submitted 35 percent fewer health care claims.

- Aetna estimates it recoups $2.70 for every dollar it spends on its lactation program.

- At Wells Fargo new mothers are returning an average of four to six weeks earlier than they did before the bank started its program in 1997.[5]

☀ *Provide nap rooms.* In Japan, many organizations provide nap rooms for their employees. You can even rent space for naps like you would a hotel room in Tokyo. The rooms have stacked cubicles almost like tanning booths that can be rented by the hour.

Research shows that taking even 15-minute nap or meditation time increases productivity substantially. Several famous inventors, writers, and industry giants were well known for their afternoon naps! Intuit Canada has three sleep rooms, each with a bed, lamp, and alarm clock. One employee said, "Few companies treat their employees this way. You'd have to drag us out kicking and screaming," and turnover is just 3 percent in an industry where 20 percent is standard.

 Provide employees with a time-out place. Employees need a place to take physical and mental breaks during their stressful workdays. Many organizations provide a quiet place for employees to read and meditate, and have access to a telephone to place local calls to family, teachers, doctors, and debtors. After I had spoken to an entire company about "Regenerating Spirit in the Workplace," a group of employees got together and found a corner cubicle area that no one was using. They stayed late one night, decorated it all in black, and the next day when the rest of the employees came to work, they found a huge computer banner over the entrance that read "The Whine Cellar!" People brought in stress toys, stuffed animals, and cartoon books, and it became everyone's favorite place to go. When anyone was crabby, coworkers simply told that person to go to the "Whine Cellar!"

 One manager gives her all-female team a morale boost by taking them to a manicure shop in the building. She explains this as "negotiating a life that keeps me coming in every morning, charged and ready to take on the world."

Hire "Moms." We all need nurturing now and then, and who better to do it than Moms? Organizations that really care about their employees can make "nurturing" part of someone's *real* job:

At Evolving Systems, Inc., a computer software company in Englewood, Colorado, they have five-and-a-half full-time "Moms" and one full-time "Dad," one *for every 80 to 90 employees. Their whole job consists in giving personal attention to the employees, and they report directly to the president of the company, Harry Fair, the originator of the Moms. Nita Cronin, whose title is Lead Mom, shared with me a little about their job, which is to create a unique, happy, friendly environment and to add the comforts of home to the workplace.*

One of their primary jobs, besides knowing each employee by name and a little bit about them and their families, is to keep all 18 kitchens (every wing in each building has 2 kitchens) stocked just as they would be at home—with dishes, silver, napkins, paper towels, fruit baskets, daily fresh fruit juices, coffee, tea, and condiments. There are also free soda and beverage-dispensing machines.

The Moms provide daily snacks, both morning and afternoon—such things like cheese and crackers, fruit plates, carrot and celery sticks, and breakfast bars—that they put out in the kitchens. They have a budget to stock the kitchens, so there is no charge to the employees for any of this. Nita said, "If employees are working and they are hungry, they break their mind-set and lose productivity if they have to go out to a convenience store, so we make it possible for them to go to the kitchen and get a small snack at any time of the day or night."

The Moms also select two restaurants a day, and they order in meals for the employees if they wish. Each employee has an account with them, so the lunch can be charged, which makes it extremely convenient. Nita says that if an employee isn't feeling well or has an injury, the Mom will deliver the lunch right to the employee's desk! The Moms provide birthday cakes at company meetings and even give employees little birthday gifts such as stress toys and balloons. They plan parties, open houses, and anniversaries and provide all types of valuable information and advice to their fellow employees.

The Moms want their office to be a fun place to be so that employees will "come to see Mom!" They stock candy, over-the-counter medications, panty hose, eyedrops, eyeglass repair kits, dental floss, toothbrushes and paste, and even shoelaces—all provided by the company. "The Mom's job is to come in with a smile and be a morale booster," says Nita. "We spend a good part of our day out and about, watering plants, saying 'Hi' to employees, inquiring about their families and hobbies, and finding out what is going on with them. When someone has a deadline, we try to drop off special treats to encourage them and thank them for their hard work, or if they aren't feeling well, we check to see how they're doing and what they might need. We even mail things for employees when they are too busy."

The company looks for warm, caring, upbeat people to be their Moms, and they are interviewed by the president himself. The philosophy of the company is, "If you can provide a good working environment, you can create better products." And that is exactly what the Moms are there to do![6]

People lose their health to make money and then lose their money to restore their health.

Kathy Brown, RN, CSP

Sponsor a wellness program. According to an article in the *Work & Family Newsbrief,* June 2002, Bank One says employees who participate in their wellness efforts cost them 18 percent less in health care expenses than those who don't.

- Citizen's Trust sponsors a *"Living Well" program,* which is "a holistic approach to health that rewards staff for the simple and good things of life—such as reading a book, visiting a parent, hugging, meditating, exercising, learning, teaching, going to the theater, etc."

- *Provide flu shots* not only for employees but also for their families. This blends work, health, and family.

- *Sponsor a Healthy Recipe Day.* Ask everyone to bring a healthy dish and share!

- *Have a healthy "Special of the Day" at your company cafeteria.*

- *Hold Caregiver Fairs.* The sponsoring company sets up the place and then invites members of the community who offer caregiving services to attend the fair at no charge. These may include retirement and assisted-living facilities, childcare groups, eldercare organizations, local hospitals, preschools, and other community representatives that could be resources for employees. The sponsoring company also gives employees work time off to attend these fairs.

Sponsor health fairs, fun runs, and charity walks. Invite employees' families to participate. When a whole family participates in a charity fundraiser such as a walk for breast cancer, they are blending work, family, health, and service!

> Men who hug and kiss their wives every morning before leaving for work live an average of five years longer, have fewer car accidents, and earn up to 30 percent more money than nonsmoochers!
>
> *Self* magazine

Provide ways to alleviate stress. Whatever the cause, stress hurts families and individuals. Of workers participating in a 1997 study by the Work Life Institute, 40 percent said they often or very often felt nervous or stressed. About 13 percent often or very often had difficulty coping with the demands of everyday life, and 26 percent often or very often felt emotionally drained by work. Another 28 percent said they had no energy for family or others, and 36 percent felt "used up" at the end of the day.[7]

 Hold classical concerts during the lunch hour once a week or once a month. This will help to relieve stress and allow employees time to concentrate on something of beauty. You might even invite employees' families to blend work, health, and family.

 Quad/Graphics, Inc., in Milwaukee, Wisconsin, offers some amazing forms of "hidden paychecks" that help relieve stress and thus greatly reduce turnover. An *on-site medical facility* offers no-cost care for employees and their families. They also offer *interest-*

free loans to purchase or repair a car, *discounted bus service* to company plants, 24-hour on-site day care, a fitness center, free legal advice, and on-site Employee Assistance Programs and tuition for education.

Many organizations are allowing employees to *buy additional vacation days or sell unused days back to the firm.* At Freddie Mac, 82 percent of employees are buying at least one extra week this year, and more than 25 percent are buying three weeks. It is promising that employees are realizing the value of taking breaks from their work. Hewitt says that despite the monetary incentive for employees to sell their leave, just 6 percent do so. Conversely, 24 percent choose to buy more vacation time.[8]

Kris Thomson, a human resources manager for Jostens, Inc., in Shelbyville, Tennessee, tells a beautiful story about how a manager recognized her stress and found an amazing way to relieve it:

A few years ago, I worked on a project (a plant consolidation—closing one down and expanding another) that took nearly a year of planning and implementing. During that year I traveled 31 weeks—from Minnesota to California—and was away from my family much of the time. At the same time I was diagnosed with a brain tumor that was successfully removed several months later. My manager was very supportive. One night when I arrived back at the airport, dead tired, she asked me to meet her at a certain place in the airport. I was apprehensive because I didn't know what it was about. My manager surprised me with a trip for me and my family (my husband and two sons) to Phoenix to visit my parents—hotel, meals, and airfare all included. We were to leave the next morning for four days. She had already contacted my husband and they had worked out all the arrangements. I was so happy I cried! This was truly one of the nicest things that anyone had ever done for me. She knew that my family was so important to me and that they and my health were taking a backseat (temporarily) to meet the needs of the project that I was a part of.

- A large bank in Boston put together *stress bags* for their managers as a fun joke. The brown paper bags were filled with small bottles of aspirin, Rolaids, bubbles, and stress balls.

- A midsize winery in Northern California passed out *lavender-filled keypad sachets* for employees to rest their wrists on when doing computer work.

- *Bring in a masseuse or masseur one day a week and give employees back and neck massages.* At the Mellon Financial Corporation offices in Philadelphia, Pennsylvania, the company has a professional come in once a month to provide back massages for employees at the rate of $1 per minute. AT&T Broadband in Englewood, Colorado, hired a local massage school to offer free *ten-minute chair massages* to its employees once a week. This was so popular that the program had to be expanded because employees quickly signed up and filled all the available spaces!

Encourage sports teams and intramurals. It is proven that exercise reduces stress, and being on a team also teaches team building. Employees often make friends with other employees from different departments when they are on the same sports team. These teams also provide healthy competition and FUN!

Hold family golf outings and baseball, softball, and soccer games. When employees' family members participate, everyone gets much needed fun and exercise, and you are blending work, family, health, and spirit.

Give employees the gift of time. What employees seem to desire more than anything else is more hours in the day to spend in their personal lives. When an organization can help them have more time available for their home lives, they are helping to alleviate stress and add more peace to the employees' hectic lives. Giving the gift of time can even increase productivity. For example, France's 35-hour workweek is BOOSTING productivity. One small jam factory had to split its 18 employees into 2 teams and now operates 4 more hours daily, producing 35 percent more than the past year with only 2 extra workers. And the bonus is that employees all have an extra 5 hours a week to do whatever they choose![9]

An article in *HR Magazine* tells about a new endeavor to help employees:

The Employee Services Management Association has announced a partnership with Service Master Home Service Center that will allow employers to offer their employees a new work-life benefit called "The Gift of Time." The new partnership has developed a service that offers contact information and gift certificates for home maintenance and

**"It's part of the company's new emphasis
on health and fitness."**

repair services. *Instead of spending weekends scrubbing, fixing, and
trimming, employees can contact and use professionals from Service Master's nine leading home-service brands to take care of needed home
repairs. Employers also can provide gift certificates for Service Master
Home Services to reward and recognize employees.*[10]

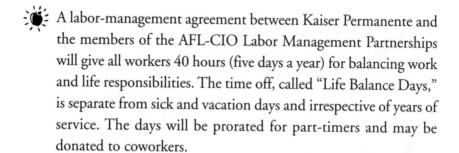

A labor-management agreement between Kaiser Permanente and the members of the AFL-CIO Labor Management Partnerships will give all workers 40 hours (five days a year) for balancing work and life responsibilities. The time off, called "Life Balance Days," is separate from sick and vacation days and irrespective of years of service. The days will be prorated for part-timers and may be donated to coworkers.

An agreement between United Auto Workers and Michigan Blue Cross Blue Shield will allow workers to take up to eight hours of paid leave in one-hour increments to participate in any educational activity, including tutoring, field trips, or classroom or preschool programs.

6

Blending Work and Spirit

Let us think of education as the means of developing our greatest abilities, because in each of us, there is a private hope and dream which, fulfilled, can be translated into benefit for everyone and greater strength for our nation.

John F. Kennedy

A GROWING INTEREST in spirituality in the workplace is evidenced by the many articles in mainstream business publications such as *Fortune, Business Week, Newsweek,* the *Wall Street Journal,* the *New York Times,* and even the *Journal of the American Medical Association.* The polls say that two out of three people have a deep yearning for spiritual growth. Half of us have experienced a personal transformation in recent years, 80 percent believe in God, 69 percent believe in the presence of angels, and 75 percent believe that unexplainable miracles are a reality in our lives.

About 90 percent reach out to the Sacred through prayer or meditation and 57 percent pray daily.[1]

These findings prove that we cannot separate our spirituality from our daily lives, and because most of us spend the bulk of our day at some kind of work, it is imperative that we find ways to blend our spirit into our worklife. When Joel and Michelle Levey, the authors of *Living in Balance,* asked the question, "When, or how, do we glimpse Spirit at work?", they heard the following reponses:

- In moments of appreciation, caring, kindness, and compassion
- In moments of deep listening, or in shared silence
- In moments of clarity, when we glimpse our place in the "big picture"
- In moments of wonder, when synchronicities converge to confirm our intuition with a "Yes!"
- In moments when we know to our core that we belong here
- In moments of creative collaboration, when we join forces to create a better world
- In mindful moments, when we are wholeheartedly present
- In moments of deep recognition of each other and of ourselves
- In moments of dialogue, when the deep listening of a group reveals a glimpse of truth larger than one person can hold
- In moments of forgiveness, when we let go of the past and focus on creating our shared future
- In moments of commitment, when our love and action blend into one[2]

Imagine yourself at work surrounded by all your coworkers, partners, customers, and suppliers. Even if we don't talk about it, the need for a renewal of spirit at work is evident.

I think we all have experienced a new awareness of spirit at work as a result of the tragedy of September 11. People found a new level of sharing and caring as they came together in their shock and grief. We can continue to experience that spirit as we share our joys with one another in the workplace and as we find our personal sense of purpose and mission in the work that we do.

In their book, *Lean and Meaningful—A New Culture for Corporate America,* Roger Herman and Joyce Gioia suggest that tomorrow's employees will not be wooed by money alone, and I have found the same thing in my work with "Regenerating Spirit in the Workplace." They believe that employees will choose employers based on their criteria of "meaningfulness." These elements of meaningfulness include:

- Work and personal life balance
- Family-centeredness
- Community involvement
- Environmental awareness
- Flexible workplace
- Personal and professional growth
- Social responsibility
- Educating tomorrow's workforce
- Spirituality
- Meaningful rewards[3]

> People need joy quite as much as clothing. Some of them need it far more.
>
> Margaret Collier Graham

Another aspect of spirit in the workplace involves having more fun at work. Because the average American spends more than half his or her life at work, our workplaces should be places of joy, places where we experience caring, creativity, purpose, and fun. Study after study shows that happy employees are more productive employees.

> Virtually anything that diverts your mind from the work at hand and gives you a few minutes of humor, relaxation, pleasure, sensory stimulation, exercise, or just plain fun will [renew your spirit].
>
> Ann McGee-Cooper, *You Don't Have to Come Home from Work Exhausted!*

In his book, *Mastering the Art of Self-Renewal: Adulthood as Continual Revitalization,* Frederic M. Hudson describes the characteristics of self-renewing adults:

1. Are value-driven.
2. Are connected to the world around them.
3. Require solitude and quiet.
4. Pace themselves.
5. Have contact with nature.
6. Are creative and playful.
7. Adapt to change.
8. Learn from their disappointments and losses.
9. Never stop learning.
10. Are future-oriented.[4]

Do these characteristics describe you? If not, the following ideas will help you renew your spirit at work.

INDIVIDUAL IDEAS

Renew your spirit in ways that help you connect with your center

 Create several two- to five-minute "joy breaks" throughout your day. Experiment with delightful little things you can do to bring yourself joy. If you have difficulty remembering to take these joy breaks, set an alarm clock or your computer to go off each hour as a signal for you to disconnect for a few minutes. Call someone who loves you, look at a magazine you enjoy, read a poem, listen to a sports score, buy yourself a treat. Do whatever brings YOU joy and then you will learn to anticipate something fun and rewarding each day at work.

Spend time daydreaming each day. Pick a time of the day, perhaps right after lunch, when you think about a happy memory. Keep a picture of yourself as a young child in your office to remind yourself of those happy, carefree times.

Create an internal checks-and-balances system that keeps the bigger picture in mind. Ask yourself, "How is my quality of life today?" Don't think about how it was yesterday or how it will be next week. Keep yourself in the present and then understand that you have choices to manage what you are doing right now.

Embrace ritual, ceremony, and art. Craig Neal, the founder of the Heartland Institute in Edina, Minnesota, suggests that you "Bring to work little aspects of who you are at home. Introduce rituals that express who you are and what you care about." He tells of an executive at a large company who started lighting a candle every time somebody came into her office. After each meeting, she'd blow the candle out. She used that ritual to set a tone—she didn't have to say why she was doing it. He says, "Make little moments of depth like this one a part of your worklife."[5]

You can create your own rituals that help you center yourself and be in touch with the present. My publisher, Cynthia Zigmund, keeps a *basket of stress toys* on her desk as a reminder not to take herself too seriously. Another executive keeps a basket of Beanie Babies and asks each person who comes into her office to choose their favorite one to hold as they talk. It is interesting to her to see what each person chooses, and it is fun for them to pick an animal that brings them comfort or joy.

The downside of going on a two-week vacation.

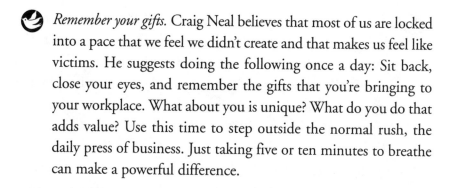

Remember your gifts. Craig Neal believes that most of us are locked into a pace that we feel we didn't create and that makes us feel like victims. He suggests doing the following once a day: Sit back, close your eyes, and remember the gifts that you're bringing to your workplace. What about you is unique? What do you do that adds value? Use this time to step outside the normal rush, the daily press of business. Just taking five or ten minutes to breathe can make a powerful difference.

Listen to motivational tapes or CDs on your way to and from work. Many lives have been changed by hearing great speakers. This uplifting experience will also help you improve your attitude when you arrive at both work and home. It is fun to start a sharing library of tapes in your office or with coworkers and then discuss at lunch what you have heard. This practice combines spirit and friends!

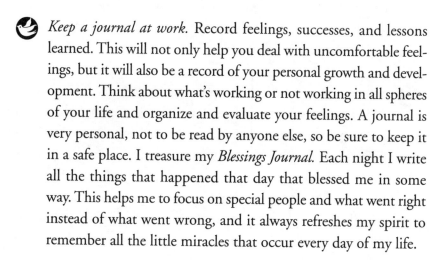

Keep a journal at work. Record feelings, successes, and lessons learned. This will not only help you deal with uncomfortable feelings, but it will also be a record of your personal growth and development. Think about what's working or not working in all spheres of your life and organize and evaluate your feelings. A journal is very personal, not to be read by anyone else, so be sure to keep it in a safe place. I treasure my *Blessings Journal.* Each night I write all the things that happened that day that blessed me in some way. This helps me to focus on special people and what went right instead of what went wrong, and it always refreshes my spirit to remember all the little miracles that occur every day of my life.

Practice centering wherever you find yourself. Whenever you have a short time with nothing to do, come back to your center. You can practice deep breathing, positive thinking, meditation, or what I call "arrow prayers" at times when you are waiting in line, on hold on the phone, waiting on a colleague, or even in a rest room!

Free up one hour a day for 30 days and use that time to reflect on a simple question: "What is it that's most complicating my life?" And then keep a journal about what you think and discover.

At work sit down with your schedule at the beginning of every month and block out time for "me." We all seem to need permission to think about ourselves, especially when we are parents of small children. It seems as if everyone needs us for something; however, if we do not take some special time to care for ourselves, we won't be much help to anybody—or at least we won't be very nice to be around! Treat time for yourself just as you would any other appointment and guard it passionately.

Schedule your recreation. Alan Zimmerman, Ph.D., CSP, says: "It's all too easy to say to your friends and family members that 'We've got to get together real soon.' But if you don't immediately ask 'When?' and put it on your calendar, it probably won't happen for weeks and weeks or months and months. My wife and I sit down four times a year to schedule our recreation. We make sure we get all the people we want to see on our calendar, and we put those fun, just-the-two-of-us getaways on the calendar as well.

We even write in our vacation weeks two years in advance." We must be as committed to recreation for our spirits as we are to our work! Remember that the root of "recreation" is "re-creation," or renewing our spirits.

> The moment one gives close attention to anything, even a blade of grass, it becomes a mysterious, awesome, indescribably magnificent world in itself.
>
> Henry Miller

Next time you get a raise, establish a direct deposit to a special savings account to be used only for "leisure blending" activities.

Use your lunch hour to renew your spirit

If you work in the city, take a *miniarchitectural tour* during your lunch hour. Visit one of the newly restored buildings or attend a free lecture.

Pamper yourself with a 30-minute *reflexology treatment or a "Facial on the Go."* Some of the spas serve a nutritious lunch while you are being cared for.

Go to an *art museum* and simply explore and absorb the beauty. Some museums offer 15-minute "Object Lessons" on particular works of art.

Find a *local health club or YMCA* and take a 45-minute class in something that would help relieve stress.

Spend your lunch hour at the *local Anticruelty Society*. It is a proven fact that playing with an animal reduces stress! You may also want to *visit a day care center* and spend time reading to or playing with the children there, especially if you don't have any of your own at home.

Find an organization you believe in to *volunteer your time one lunch hour a week*. Many groups are delighted to accommodate busy schedules.

Attend a *cooking class or a style show* at a nearby department store.

Go to a *local park* and spend some time playing on the playground equipment. Do you still know how to pump yourself up on the swings?

Go to the *local library* and get lost in the stacks. Many also offer free lectures during the lunch hour.

Many cultural centers in large cities provide *free musical concerts* during the lunch hour. Often they feature new, up-and-coming young artists.

Celebrate others to renew both their spirits and your own. When we bring happiness into the lives of others, we cannot help feeling good ourselves. Whenever I am really having a down day, I take a few minutes and write "love" notes to people who have blessed me in some way or I wrap little gifts to give or mail to those I want to specially remember. It is such fun to think about surprising people that it almost always gets me out of my own misery!

Think about how you have treated others around you. If you could review recent conversations with your spouse, coworkers, children, and people in general, would you find your input into their lives uplifting? What would the overall effect of your words be?

Do you have a tendency to notice others' failures rather than the many things they do well? Neva Coyle said, "Our job is not to straighten each other out, but to help each other up." I encourage you to be more appreciative of people. That habit will renew your spirit more than just about anything. Almost everyone values a compliment, encouragement, or a little recognition now and then. We simply need to develop an eye for discovering what is right about a person and then actively seek ways to express appreciation for the good traits we find. I love the quotation from William Winter: "As much of Heaven is visible as we have eyes to see." Begin today looking with your heavenly eyes!

Does this thought from Albert Schweitzer describe your interactions with others:

"Sometimes our light goes out but is blown again into flame by an encounter with another person. Each of us owes the deepest thanks to those who have rekindled this inner light."

> Mindfulness is the practice of aiming your attention, moment to moment, in the direction of your purpose. It is called mindfulness because you have to keep your purpose in mind as you watch your attention. Then, whenever you notice that your aim has drifted off, you calmly realign it.
>
> Frank Andrews

"I tell ya, meals used to be such a pain in the neck! Now, thanks to the vending machines, they're a breeze. No more cooking, no more dirty dishes. ..."

Write a Balanced Mission Statement. Think about all the roles you play in your life.

Do you:

- Have a job?
- Have a spouse or significant other?
- Have children at home?
- Have elderly parents?
- Have a social life?
- Participate in an exercise program?
- Have a hobby?
- Belong to a religious organization?
- Volunteer for your church or community?
- Believe strongly in one or two causes?

Susan Iida-Pederson, the vice president of corporate relations for Creative Memories, talks about the importance of writing a balanced mission statement. She says it is important to know who we are and what we value. That way when we find ourselves in "fast-forward," we can hit "pause" and remember that what we do is secondary to who we are. Then we can focus less on our "to do" list and more on our "to be" list. Writing a balanced mission statement is a part of blending our spirit with the other aspects of our lives.

To begin your own Balanced Mission Statement, first list each of the six areas of your life:

1. **WORK**
2. **FAMILY**
3. **FRIENDS**
4. **HEALTH**
5. **SPIRIT**
6. **SERVICE**

For each area express in one or two phrases or a sentence what you value about that area or what you want to be in that part of your life. Then put these sentences or phrases together to form your Balanced Mission Statement. Here is an example from Rhonda Ellis, a senior director for Creative Memories: "I want to contribute to a happy, loving, encouraging family and maintain a peaceful, secure home . . . to operate a profitable, part-time business . . . to grow in God's wisdom and reflect this to others . . . to encourage and mentor others, especially women . . . and I want to be strong in character and gentle in spirit."

As you think about each area, consider these questions:

WORK—Is this about income, an entrepreneurial spirit, security, sharing with others? Is it a creative or social outlet, a personal development opportunity, the application of a gift or talent? Do you have a sense of mission about your work? What do you value or want to be in your work?

FAMILY—What do you value for your family—harmony, peace, quality time, love, respect, fun, communication, caring for others? What is important to you about your home—order, hospitality, comfort, joyfulness? Do you value quiet, peace, and serenity, or activity, energy, and community?

FRIENDS—What value do you place on friends in your life? What kind of relationships do you want to have and what kind of friend do you want to be?

HEALTH—What value do you place on your health? How do you want to live and care for yourself?

SPIRIT—Is spirit to you about God, prayer, and reflection? Or is it about being ethical, moral, loving, forgiving, or generous, being a person of grace? Do you value doing the right thing, spending time in church or a synagogue, helping others, inner peace? Do you value education, lifelong learning, using your gifts? Do you value the joy of living each day to the fullest? What do you want to be in this area of your life?

SERVICE—Are you passionate about a cause? Do you feel a need to give back to the world? Where do you want to make a difference?

Notice if you had difficulty clarifying any of these six areas of your life. Often this exercise will help us to see which areas of our lives we might have been neglecting.

Finally, define the essence of who you are as a person. This is about character traits such as integrity, caring, honesty, enthusiasm. Are you task-minded, free-spirited, and adventurous, or are you conservative, quiet, and thoughtful? What do you want to be as a person? What traits do you value most?

Now, how do you apply this Balanced Mission Statement to your work and to your life? Susan Iida-Pederson suggests that to make it an effective working document, it needs two other pieces: goals, based on your mission, and a calendar schedule. Pick two mission areas to focus on each quarter and set goals for them. As you reach these goals, replace them with new quarterly goals. She emphasizes the importance of scheduling an hour on your calendar each quarter to assess current goals and plan new goals for the upcoming quarter. As you begin to meet these goals, you will be regenerating your spirit!

Start support groups to encourage sharing spirituality at work

 In an article in the *Boston Globe* by Diane E. Lewis titled "Spiritual revival revealed in workplace—Some workers seek more than just a job," Carol Ross, a retention leader and organizational development professional at Avaya, a New Jersey computer systems software firm, *started a luncheon series titled, "Bringing Forth Soul in the Workplace,"* after her company had gone through an emotionally draining restructuring experience. She brought soothing music, encouraged meditation, and invited inspirational speakers to the lunches. After losing 20 percent of their staff, people were drained. Not only did they have more work, but they also had lost their friends, so their world was turned upside down. These luncheons helped people make sense of the change.[6]

 Send an inspirational e-mail every Monday to your fellow employees. We all need to be reminded of positive things, especially on Monday morning! Starting the week in good spirits will make a difference the rest of our days at work.

 Start a spiritual book study in your organization. Robin Maynard organized a Bible study with her coworkers at Land O Lakes called "Women of Balance." Similar groups have been started in many workplaces since September 11 to help people cope with the tragedy and find purpose and value in their lives and work. These study groups can be based on spirit-lifting books of any faith.

Create a "comfort drawer" for yourself at work. In her book *The Simple Abundance Companion,* Sarah Ban Breathnach suggests creating a drawer at work that brings you solace and serenity and a feeling of safety and joy. Fill your drawer with things that bring you comfort and make you feel cared for—aspirin, extra panty hose, a sewing kit. Then add foods or treats that are special to you—herbal teas, your favorite candy bars, truffles, or hard candy, smells that make you smile, pictures of people and things you love, stuffed animals that remind you of someone or something dear to you, beautiful writing paper or notepaper, special thoughts, Bible verses, or quotations, special skin creams, scented candles, CDs that bring you peace, and even whimsical things such as packets of glitter or cute stickers.[7]

Do fun things at work. We all take ourselves far too seriously. Research shows that the most productive workplaces enjoy at least ten minutes of laughter an hour. Even under the greatest stress, humor is important. Use your imagination and create your own fun that will work in your culture.

Enjoy some playtime at work each day. Just as you make the time to work, you have to make the time to play. Do you remember the children's song lyrics, "If you're happy and you know it, clap your hands"? If I asked you that today, would you be clapping? Right now list all the ways YOU like to play. Can you even remember how? Think about how children play for the fun of feeling good, not to measure their performance. Bring several items to your workplace that encourage you to play—Nerf balls, clapping hands, clown noses, dolls, sports equipment, noisemakers. We need to laugh, to return to the joyfulness and freedom of our inner child and renew our spirits.

 In her book *You Don't Have to Go Home from Work Exhausted!,* Ann McGee-Cooper suggests that we *make a part of every lunch something fun for the little kid within,* "perhaps a few minutes to browse in a bookstore, a brisk walk to enjoy the flowers in a mall, just pushing back to relax . . . whatever would give you a lift and a break from all the pressure and push." I love to read catalogs when I am eating lunch. Then they don't pile up at home, and I don't have to feel guilty![8]

 Personalize your workspace. Photographs of family, pets, favorite vacations, art, a comfortable chair, something from you favorite hobby—all these touches make a home out of this part of your life. You deserve all the nurturing you can provide. My office is my "place of JOY!" It is filled with things that renew my spirit: a photograph of Mother Teresa, one of the people who has most influenced my life; several huge collages my daughter made for me that contain cards, notes, and letters, as well as photos from my audience members over the years; several pieces of art that were handmade just for me by special people in my life; a small picture from a precious speaking trip to Greece; a memento from the University of Kansas where I went to school; a teddy bear, a magic wand, and many kinds of items with butterflies, given to me by dear friends and clients; seashells to remind me of the ocean that has been so healing in my life; many, many books, most of which are signed by the authors who are professional friends of mine; a plaque recording the number of miles I have swum each summer at our community pool; and a clear plastic desk cover under which I've placed dozens of my favorite quotations and Bible verses.

> **The more and more you listen, the more and more you will hear. The more you hear, the more and more deeply you will understand.**
>
> Jamyang Kyentse
> Rinpoche

Be a lifelong learner. Five minutes a day spent growing intellectually may not seem like much, but that adds up to more than 30 hours a year of personal "class time."

 Participate in classes and seminars that you have an interest in.

 Ask your boss to attend a class or seminar with you.

 Negotiate taking a college class on company time, *one that will benefit both you and your company.*

"Hold on gang let me make sure I've got everything. Beeper, check. Laptop, check. Cellular phone, check. Boy, I can hardly wait to get to the beach and relax."

Visibly demonstrate the results of classes or training in your work. Show your manager what difference a class or seminar has made in your life. Then you will more likely be allowed to attend more.

Read a new book each month. I always have three going at a time— one spiritual, one business, and one for pure enjoyment! If you read one book each month, you're in the company of the top 1 percent of the intellectuals in America. It is amazing how much time you can find to read during a workday if you use lunchtime, waiting time, and commuting time (if you take public transportation).

Attend a lecture with a coworker who stimulates you. Talk about what you learned. This is blending work, spirit, and friends.

Create an environment conducive to learning. Surround yourself with good books, play stimulating music, and keep your desk stocked with study supplies, and don't be afraid to go back to school.

Ask questions of those around you. Always be learning!

Continue to question, *"What can I learn from this experience?"*

Share your talents and gifts

Create a hobby exchange. Find a place in your break room or cafeteria and display one person's hobby each week or each month. This will not only encourage others and create networking, but it will also celebrate the gifts of your coworkers.

Volunteer to teach others something that you are good at. This sharing can provide great bartering in the workplace as well as create new networking relationships.

Help foster an atmosphere that encourages positive spirit

 Linda Katz, the manager of Colleague Shared Services at Adecco in Melville, New York, says, "I hold meetings every other week with my staff and have begun the following program: Each meeting one team member is chosen to do a *team-building exercise with the group* to start the meeting. I started by buying holiday lollipops before Easter/Passover. I asked each team member to take one lollipop and pass it to the person next to him or her. Before they gave the lollipops to these persons, they were to say something nice to them such as a compliment or a "thank you" for something that those persons had done for them. It was fun and even made the cranky people a bit happier!"

 Rosemary Thomas of the Mellon Financial Corporation in Philadelphia, Pennsylvania, holds a *weekly group meeting* with the Employee Assistance Program specialists to talk about whatever is concerning people. Just getting these topics out in the open helps change the atmosphere.

 Nicole Tefft, the executive director of human resources for St. Catherine Hospital in Garden City, Kansas, shares how they create a positive spirit: "We have a *prayer every morning and wish people happy birthdays.* We also *recognize Service Excellence recipients over the public-address system,* and *every time a baby is born, we play a short medley of lullabies.*"

ORGANIZATIONAL IDEAS

Encourage employees' special interests. In my book *Handle with CARE—Motivating and Retaining Employees,* I shared many ways that different organizations are participating in recognizing and celebrating employees as unique human beings with lives outside of work. This kind of sharing builds relationships across the organization as well as encourages creative spirits.

- Gates Rubber Company, Denver, Colorado, *holds art shows on-site,* where employees can display and sell their work to fellow employees and to the public. Other companies, such as Jet Propulsion Labs, encourage art by offering discount tickets to art museums and art galleries.

- Jet Propulsion Labs' recreation club in Pasadena, California, *formed a music club* in which instrument-playing employees hold jam sessions with others interested in similar styles of music. Specialty bands such as jazz and rock are formed within this club, and the members have a wonderful opportunity for extra practice and sharing their special talents. Other companies sponsor company choirs and drama teams. They often perform at all-company functions.

- Compaq Computers, Houston, Texas, holds a *creative photo contest* in several different categories with incentives for the winners. Other organizations start photography clubs.

Schulmerich Bells in Sellersville, Pennsylvania, decided to initiate an activity that would draw together people from various parts of the company. Their answer was clear—*a handbell choir.* They perform six times a year at senior centers and nursing homes during the noon hours.[9]

 Another example is University of California–San Francisco—Empact! They have a *poetry group* for enthusiasts to share their work and to get feedback. Poetry readings are held at a library where a public audience is invited to hear the voices of these poets, young and old.

Encourage employees to find quiet times in their day. Joel and Michelle Levey in their book *Living in Balance* discuss the importance of living "mindfully," becoming aware of what we are doing and thinking and feeling in each moment of time. In that way we discover that we have choices. They share how in numerous organizations teams have *adopted a bell or chime of mindfulness* that is rung at random times of the day as a reminder for people to take a moment to come back to themselves, to their centers: "Each day the bell is passed to another person in the office, and as the gently melodious sound of the bell echoes out through the floor, people are invited to take a deep breath, to focus their mind and let it shine." They say the greatest strategy they have to offer whenever one is feeling particularly frazzled, scattered, and out of balance is simply to return to the awareness of one's breathing. "Like an anchor in the midst of a stormy sea, breath awareness is a balancing force for the mind, anchoring you in the present."[10]

Encourage personal growth and development

Provide various kinds of workshops for employees that will impact their personal lives. Schedule workshops to improve home-time management and communication, deal with guilt, and conduct marriage and financial planning seminars. As you help employees feel better about themselves and their lives outside of work, they will have more positive energy to spend on the job.

EPCOR, a large Canadian utilities company, believes in career development and *pays for courses,* especially toward getting a university degree. They have a turnover rate of 5 percent and are such a popular company to work for that they won't accept unsolicited résumés.[11]

In 1999 the United Auto Workers focused primarily on work-life issues when negotiating a new collective bargaining agreement with Ford Motor Company and Visteon Corporation, an independent auto parts manufacturer. UAW officials chose "Bargaining for Families" as the theme of the negotiations. The final contract agreement created a *program called the Family Service and Learning Centers* that will offer programs in more than 30 U.S. locations in three categories: family education and services; early childhood education services; and community service, education, and outreach. Their intention is to provide cutting-edge opportunities for personal growth and development for their members.[12]

A banker recently invited his department to a *career management seminar.* In doing so, he told them, "You've given us a significant investment of your time. Now it's time to invest in yourself. Take this day to think about your work and your life and how you can be as satisfied and meaningfully engaged as possible."

Start book clubs in your office. Invite coworkers to read the same book and then get together once a month to discuss it. At Citizens Trust, a *monthly reading group* discusses works of fiction. Citizens covers half the cost of the books, buys pizza, and provides a "relaxation room" for the group to meet after work hours.

Begin a mentoring program. One of the best ways to create a unified spirit in your workplace is to provide coaches and guides for newer employees.

"Here's how it works: If the ball hits the floor in your cubicle, you've gotta be on call for the weekend."

Focus on working fathers. James Levine, the director of the Father-hood Project at the Families and Work Institute, says, "We've focused for the past two decades on working mothers, but we haven't even developed a concept of the working father." Marriott International has launched two initiatives to teach fathers from different parts of the company how to lead richer lives with their families. One is "Effective Fathering," a course aimed at frontline employees. The other is "Daddy Stress/Daddy Success," a seminar that targets executives. Both raise questions that every working father should ask himself:

1. *Do you know what your kids want?* Levine's group conducted in-depth research on what children want from working parents. "We suspected that what kids wanted was more time, but what they actually wanted was for their parents to be *less stressed*"—even if that meant the parents spent less time with them. "You can't help your kids unless you help yourself," Levine argues.

2. *Do you have the tools of the fatherhood trade?* Little things count for a lot!

Marriott's program is wildly popular. They have had a greater demand for these courses than they have had for any other.[13]

> A rich person is not one who has the most but is the one who needs the least.
>
> Kathy Brown, RN, CSP

Provide spiritual support for employees. According to the Fellowship for Companies for Christ, approximately 10,000 Bible and prayer groups across America meet on a regular basis. Buddhist reading groups are also growing in popularity.

After the exposure of the corporate greed of the 1980s, many people decided that they would no longer check their personal values at the company door. As a result of September 11, many people have reevaluted their goals, their lives, and their values, and church attendance, volunteerism, and service work has increased. Likewise, many organizations are becoming more aware of and supporting employees' spiritual needs. Here are some of the things organizations can do:

- *Provide special places for quiet time.* At Avaya, a New Jersey computer systems software firm, there is a special room for prayer and meditation.

- *Encourage prayer and meditation groups.* At Children's Hospital Medical Center in Cincinnati, Ohio, a registered nurse uses meditation and team building to create a more inclusive work environment. She is now developing spiritual retreats for the hospital's intensive care cardiac unit.

- *Offer study classes on religious books.* Bible classes are available on a personal choice basis at Interstate Battery Company in Dallas, Texas. Other companies provide study groups for several different religions.

- *Hire chaplains. Fortune* magazine reports that companies such as Taco Bell, Pizza Hut, and Wal-Mart are now hiring Army-style chaplains who minister to any religious flavor desired. Members of these 24-hour "God Squads" visit the sick, deal with nervous breakdowns, respond to suicide attempts, and officiate at weddings and funeral services for company employees. More and more employees are no longer willing to tolerate "disconnection" between what they do for a living and what they value and believe in.[14]

An article in the Travel section of *Entrepreneur* magazine by Christopher Elliott tells how airports are enabling business travelers to practice what they preach:

Balancing a life on the road with a walk of faith can be a struggle for business travelers, but airports are trying to help. Last year, for instance, the Albany Airport in New York opened a new terminal with a dedicated interfaith prayer room *developed with the help of local religious leaders, as did Washington's Reagan National Airport. Larger facilities, such as Chicago's O'Hare International Airport, offer formal services on holy days.*[15]

Providing people with a quiet place for meditation is important in airports, according to the Airports Council International.

Covenant Transport, Inc., a nationwide trucking company, brings the religious beliefs of its founder and chief executive, David Parker, into its business. Expressions of faith range from *voluntary prayer meetings and Bible studies* at company headquarters to the *biblical scroll on its truck trailers.* A growing number of workers are looking for spiritual involvement on the job because they have issues with the lack of integrity they see in the workplace and they're looking for a company that is operating according to spiritual principles. Even those who do not agree with the company's religious outlook value their reputation as an honest company.

Recently the company provided a room at headquarters for a Muslim driver to pray, reflecting the increasingly diverse work-force in America.[16]

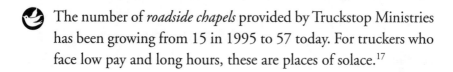 The number of *roadside chapels* provided by Truckstop Ministries has been growing from 15 in 1995 to 57 today. For truckers who face low pay and long hours, these are places of solace.[17]

Promote a caring environment

Encourage ethical standards. The company credo at the Container Store in Dallas, Texas, is based on the Golden Rule: Employees are obligated to treat customers as they would like themselves treated.

Celebrate one another. Plan "You Are Special" days for various departments. Let employees know how much they are valued and appreciated. One of my client's departments hosted a special luncheon for each of its internal customer departments to thank them for their support. Each luncheon had a theme and included some fun, interactive games.

Have empathy for coworkers' needs. United Parcel Service has started a program of weekly calls to see if employees with deployed relatives might need a hand, whether that means helping with financial matters for a spouse or mowing the lawn of elderly parents.

Bring in comfort foods. In a down economy workplaces can be depressing and cause everybody to feel blue. This reduces overall productivity and gets in the way of teamwork, creativity, and problem solving. When a manager brings in a treat, employees feel uplifted and appreciated. One manager says she has been *buying bagels* on the way into work in the morning and passing them out to her team. She says that everyone really seems to appreciate this simple gesture. Bioware, a Canadian video game maker, starts each day with an *impressive continental breakfast spread.* Feeding employees' lighter side with food, cartoons, motivational sayings, and fun often goes a long way in letting employees know you care.

Create a human-level database. Start a database of all the things employees love to do outside of work: what hobbies and interests people have; who has traveled where; who speaks a language; who plays an instrument or sings; who follows certain sports teams; who loves opera, ballet, theater, or dance; who is an artist, etc. It is amazing to find out the diversity and uniqueness of your employees, and armed with this kind of information companies can encourage all types of common-interest groups to form in their workplaces.

Hold a "bring your pet to work" day. New research shows that petting an animal is a great stress reliever, and people who have pets live longer than those who don't. For many employees without children, pets are the most important things in their lives and providing a way to share them with their coworkers can be a real spirit booster. If bringing the real animal may be disruptive or cause problems with your building's management, hold a *"Bring a Picture of Your Pet" day* at work!

Celebrate successes. At the end of a large project or a busy season, *provide a catered lunch.* You may even decide to make it a surprise. Anything you do to show you appreciate your employees will automatically boost their spirits.

In her article "7 Tips to Put Some 'Life' into Your Workday," consultant, speaker, and author Mary Nestor shares these ideas[18]:

Get Lost! Bring your favorite book, crossword puzzle, craft project, etc., to get lost in while you're eating your lunch. Whether you knit, needlepoint, or solve brainteasers for fun, getting lost in an activity completely removed from work is a great "brain break" and can refresh the mind and soul for the rest of the day.

Get Out! Lots of companies maintain picnic tables or other outdoor rest areas. Take your lunch outside and watch the birds or clouds, or talk with a friend. Pack a picnic—a hot dog and bun to microwave, chips, soft drink, watermelon chunks, and your favorite cake snack. Add a red checkered paper napkin, and you're all set.

Trip Out! An art aficionado? Homeless advocate? Mountain climber? Find a poster that depicts where your interests or passions lie and display it in your work area. When the day gets hectic, take a moment and put yourself in the poster—strolling leisurely through the art museum, scaling the peak, or raising walls at the Habitat for Humanity homesite. Feel stress fade away as you take a virtual minivacation. When you return, you'll be refreshed and ready to take on the rest of the day.

Chill Out! Pass on the regular lunch session with your coworkers. Find a quiet spot to think, plan, or write down your thoughts in

"Now what have I told you? *Never* bother Mommy
when she's in the bathroom!"

a journal. Close your office door (if you have one) or find an empty conference room, put your feet up, and take a power nap. Plan your next vacation or write a poem, some letters, or thank-you notes. Make a list of all your blessings. Call someone you haven't spoken to in a long while and let them know how special they are to you.

Encourage sabbaticals and time off. According to a recent national poll, nearly seven in ten people who make more than $40,000 a year fantasize about taking a few months off from work. And one out of every five 35- to 49-year-olds fantasizes about it daily. Some are simply burned out and yearn to check out of the pressure cooker and recoup, while others long to fulfill a long-held dream. Taking time off in this economy sounds crazy, but some companies use this as a way to keep loyal and productive employees. In fact, a whopping 70 percent of Fortune 500 companies offer some type of leave policy. Traditional sabbaticals for colleges and universities have been around for a long time. Now some worker-friendly companies also see the advantages of giving their employees a break. Ideally, a sabbatical should be an opportunity to stretch yourself, to learn something new.

Bonnie Rubin Miller, author of *Time Out: How to Take a Year (or More or Less) Off without Jeopardizing Your Job, Your Family, or Your Bank Account,* says that about 14 percent of U.S. companies have a formal sabbatical policy, and others may be amenable to an employee's proposal for one if the right case were made. Steps to take to sell your employer include[19]:

1. Check with Human Resources or in your benefits information package to see if your company has an official policy on leaves of absence.

2. Assess your personal goals for the time away and determine how much time you need and whether you have the financial means to take unpaid leave.
3. Consider the benefits to your company, how the time away will make you a better employee.
4. Develop a plan for how your work will get done without incurring much additional cost.
5. Put your proposal in writing, focusing on the benefits to the company and solutions to the concerns management might have about your absence.

The Society for Human Resource Management (SHRM) found that in 2000, 17 percent of employers offered paid sabbaticals.[20] Catalyst, a New York research firm, discovered that 18 percent of Generation Xers currently take leaves and sabbaticals whether paid or not. More and more corporations are finding that offering sabbaticals can increase productivity, enhance creativity, instill loyalty, and keep employees working for the organization longer.

Apple Computer offers a *six-week paid sabbatical after every five years of employment.*

The Frank Russell Company gives employees *eight weeks of paid time after ten or more years of full-time employment.*

Wells Fargo Bank has a *Volunteer Leave program* in which employees can take up to six months of paid leave as well as a *Personal Growth Leave program,* which is paid up to three months.

Eastman Kodak offers a *leave program called Unique Personal Opportunities* that allows employees an unpaid leave of absence of up to one year to pursue whatever they would like, including maternity and paternity leave.

More and more companies are preaching the concept of work-life balance and encouraging employees to view life more holistically and make time for relationships outside of work. Several companies are sending executives on *"silent retreats"* where they have a chance to retreat from the constant pull of technology and reflect.

A small bank in Marin County, California, gives all employees *every other Friday afternoon off* to spend with family or friends.

Take an "on-the-job sabbatical." Linda Manassee Buell, a life coach and author in Poway, California, whose Web site is <www.simplifylife.com>, suggests several things to do to reduce stress and take minisabbaticals:

- Take *breathing breaks.* Sit down, stare at a spot on the wall, and focus for five minutes on your breathing, keeping your mind free from thinking about problems.
- Instead of the radio, play a *CD of soothing music.*
- *Eat regularly.*
- *Keep a good book on hand* at all times for a special "time-out." Have distractions that help you escape.
- Keep a *vase of fresh flowers* on your desk.
- *Shut your door for 30 minutes* a day to go through paperwork without interruption.

Bonnie Michaels, president of Managing Work and Family and author of *A Journey of Work-Life Renewal: The Power to Recharge and Rekindle the Passion in Your Life,* recently took a year's sabbatical and gives this advice:

Tips for a Short-term Sabbatical

- *Determine what you need. Depending on the stage of your life and career, you will want to evaluate what will help you get renewed. Be creative.*
- *Research your organization (human resources, benefits, or the grapevine). Find out what the policy is for time off. If you are the first, find a comparable organization that has a policy. Locate an individual who has successfully negotiated a similar time away.*
- *Develop a plan that fits the cycle of work—don't plan a sabbatical at the busiest time of the year. Show the benefits. Put your proposal in writing.*
- *Anticipate some negative responses and be well prepared with answers.*
- *Have a clear plan if you are turned down. What are you willing to live with?*
- *Be creative with financing the trip. Volunteer work costs very little. Remember that renewal is like putting oil in your car. Without it, you will go dry!*

7

Blending Work and Service

There is no idea so uplifting as the idea of service to humanity.

Woodrow Wilson

IN AN ARTICLE by Cedric B. Johnson, Ph.D., in *The Inner Edge* magazine, April/May 2000, titled "When Working Harder Is *Not* Smarter," the author shares a checklist for a "fruitful" person. He believes, based on current research, that the reason for a business besides just profit is to meet the deeper needs of its employees to not simply be productive, but to be fruitful. He believes that three aspects of persons need to be expressed in their work: *nous* (mind), *psyche* (the instincts and emotions), and *pneuma* (spirit). Fruitful people are those who effectively engage all three levels in their work.

The rational part of our being is inspired by the content of our job and the opportunity to choose our mission at work. People love to engage, expand, and challenge their minds, and this level operates best when there is a program of lifelong education in an organization.

The instincts and emotions of our being are often the unconscious part of our nature that is engaged and expressed by the passion we have for our work. The sheer excitement about the job and the opportunity to collaborate with others drives us through obstacles and discouragement to accomplish much more than we realize possible.

The spirit of the person, often neglected or disregarded, is "the capacity of humanity that causes us to reach for principles and a power beyond ourselves." We can also describe spirit as the ethical type of character who finds a calling in his or her work, who sees that work as making a difference for good in the lives of others. This sense of calling or spirit gives a person's life deeper meaning through his or her work.

Here is a checklist for a "fruitful" person:

In the area of *nous* (the mind)
- There are ample opportunities for intellectual growth.
- My opinions are valued and taken into account.
- My curiosity is continually stimulated.
- Creativity is encouraged and rewarded.
- I am encouraged to come up with new ideas.
- I have uninterrupted time to think deeply.
- I have a clear career development plan.
- I know, or am willing to learn, how to get the job done.
- I am continually learning in the work I do.

In the area of *psyche* (the instincts and emotions)
- My instincts are attended to by myself and others.
- I like working with my colleagues, clients, or customers.

- I am grateful to be a part of a collaborative effort.
- I am seldom bored at work.
- The work environment is exciting.
- I feel joy at work.
- I feel gratified that my contribution is recognized.
- I share in the rewards of corporate success.
- I feel loyalty to the company, clients, or customers.
- I am proud of what I do.

In the area of *pneuma* (the spirit)
- Business is conducted by the Golden Rule.
- My values are in harmony with the company's.
- I am of service to others.
- I am making a contribution to society as a whole.
- I draw strength from my highest self or a transcendent source.
- I have a deep sense of meaning or calling in the work that I do.
- I am energized by my spiritual principles and practices.
- I have found a home for my calling in the company's mission.
- I have reverence for the environment.

How many of these can you answer as "TRUE" in your work? Dr. Johnson says, "Perhaps now you have the tools to evaluate your own work situation. Are you overworked but unproductive? Are you productive but unfruitful? How well do you integrate the three aspects of your persona in fruitful work? What specific steps do

> We cannot do great things in life; we can only do small things with great love.
>
> Mother Teresa

you need to make toward fruitfulness? As you begin to imagine pos-sibilities of fruitfulness, plan and act toward that end, and you will experience the 'flow' where you enjoy the job for itself and not just the pay. A new energy will fill you where work hours will fly by. Your self-consciousness and fear of failure will evaporate. Is this just a fanciful dream? On the contrary, it is the experience of all who enjoy a life of fruitfulness."[1]

INDIVIDUAL IDEAS

Include your family in the work-sponsored service projects you individually choose to support. This blends work, service, AND family.

 When our son, Garrett, was in junior high school, my husband decided to *participate in an inner-city tutoring program* sponsored by his employer. Each Tuesday evening the tutors took a van to a church in the inner city where they worked with elementary students on school subjects such as reading and math. One evening my husband invited Garrett to come along. Garrett was so touched by the plight of these young, underprivileged children that he asked his Dad if he could help, too. Once a week for that entire year Charlie and Garrett spent the evening together, along with other volunteers, helping children learn. What a wonderful way to share your values with a child as well as your coworkers!

 One night a month *organize a service project for families in your department.* This could involve helping at a food bank, serving meals at a shelter, or assisting the elderly.

Ask coworkers to participate in "Operation Christmas Child" or a similar organization. Samaritan's Purse is a nonprofit relief organization that sponsors a project to reach out to needy children around the world by sending them shoe box gifts. Here are the instructions:

1. Find an empty shoe box.
2. Decide whether your gift will be for a boy or a girl and their age category: (2–4), (5–9), or (10–14). Use an appropriate label that can be obtained by calling 800-353-5949.
3. Fill the box with a variety of gifts using the organization's suggestions. You may enclose a note to the child and a photo.
4. Enclose $5 and put it inside your shoe box to help cover shipping and other costs. Then place a rubber band around your box and lid.
5. For the collection center nearest your organization, call 800-353-5949 or you can mail the shoe box to:

   Samaritan's Purse
   Operation Christmas Child
   801 Bamboo Road
   P.O. Box 3000
   Boone, NC 28607

This is just one example of the dozens of charities you and your organization can easily participate in.

 Start a volunteer program in your organization to read to children at risk. Invite whole families to participate in this effort. Anyone who can read can enjoy the experience of sharing a book with another person.

Set a family goal to "adopt" another family at work or in your community. If every functional family would take an active interest in one other family or one child at risk, it could make a huge difference in our communities.

Share vacation time with those in need. One of my clients had a young mother on the staff whose husband was dying of a brain tumor. When her vacation days had run out, people who did not even know her donated their days so that she could spend the last weeks of her husband's life at his side. At UC–Davis, part of the University of California system, when an administrator had recurring breast cancer and used up her own leave time, the assistant dean in her department sent out an e-mail requesting help. The response was thrilling—people who didn't even know her donated their precious vacation time, and they accumulated a year of leave time.

Help with childcare and/or eldercare in your organization

 If your company has a day care center, now and then *go by and rock or feed the babies, play with the children, or even read to them for a few minutes.* Not only will this be a delightful stress reliever for you (especially if you do not have any children in the day care center!), but it will also give the children some individual attention and provide the day care staff with a small break.

 If your organization has an eldercare facility, *spend a few minutes each week* sharing lunch with the participants, recording their stories, or writing letters for them. Your life will be much richer for the experience and they will have a new friend. If your facility does not have a day care or eldercare center, you could also spend time with a coworker's child or parent during your lunch hour.

Start a tutoring program. This could be a program for the community, for disadvantaged children, or even for employees of your own company. When you are serving, it does not matter who you serve. The only thing that matters is your attitude of doing something for someone else. Think about the question, What would I like to teach someone?

Represent your company at a local school on Career Day. This not only serves the local school and the children enrolled, but it also creates good public relations for your organization.

Begin an Intergenerational Sharing Program. When our three children were in Field Park School in Western Springs, Illinois, I volunteered to start an Intergenerational Sharing Program. I spent several months talking with many adults in the community, especially retired people, interviewing them about what hobbies and interests they had that they could share with a group of young people. I found folks who had interesting hobbies like woodworking, baking, gardening, crafts, and music. Other adults were willing to teach cheerleading and languages, to share travel information and interesting things about other cultures, and some even wanted to read to the children. One parent offered to take a group on a tour of O'Hare Airport where he worked, and another father who owned a landscaping business volunteered to let the children learn about many of his large pieces of equipment.

We created a list of all the activities that different adults had volunteered to lead, and each child in the grade school got a first, second, and third choice. I then worked out the choices so that all the children got one of their three choices and many of them got their first choice. Each quarter the children had new choices. Then for three consecutive Thursdays for 45 minutes immediately after school, the children spent time in small groups, usually just three or four children with an adult in one of the interest groups, and each child spent time with four different adults during the school year.

Although it took time to organize initially, the program was highly successful. Both the adults and the children enjoyed the experiences, and many lasting relationships were formed between an older person and a child. The sharing created much goodwill in the community and gave both generations a better understanding of and relationship with each other. I also found that many retired people in the community were delighted to be able to share their knowledge and experiences who had never been asked, and it was a gift for them to feel useful and important as well as for the children who got to make a new friend.

This program could easily be adapted to a work environment, and could also include retired employees who would have more time. It could be scheduled for the end of a workday at a local school, using employees as volunteers. If you would like more information on how to go about setting up such a program, e-mail me at bglanz@barbaraglanz.com.

Create a community garden at work. This project could have many service benefits—beautifying the area, providing food for the disadvantaged, or simply furnishing a team-building experience for those who love to garden! To blend even more areas of your life, ask family and friends to help get it started.

Be a judge for a community or professional activity. If your expertise is in giving presentations, volunteer to be a judge for a speech contest. If you are scientifically inclined, judge a science fair. If you like to write, help with an essay contest in your community. Using your professional expertise in ways that will help others not only serves the members of your community, but it also offers a positive image for your organization.

Give blood at work. This is one of the easiest ways to serve your fellowman and your community.

Coach kids' teams or lead scout troops or clubs. As a coach or leader, you will both serve and learn new skills and practice new behaviors that will benefit your worklife. When a senior executive started coaching his son's basketball team, he learned to explain each player's step-by-step

> One of the finest sides to living is liking people and wanting to share activities in the human enterprise. The greatest pleasures come by giving pleasure to those who work with us, the person who lives next door, and to those who live under the same roof. Entering into this human enterprise, feeling oneself a part of the community, is a very important element that generates happiness.
>
> Fred J. Hafling

role in reaching objectives. Using the same skills at work made a huge difference in the executive's communication techniques. As a manager works with young people, he or she can learn vitally important coaching skills that can encourage and transform employees while at the same time the manager is serving his or her community.

ORGANIZATIONAL IDEAS

Plan service projects that involve families. When an organization does this, they blend work, service, AND family, and at the same time they are modeling the value of service to others.

 Volunteering is high-quality family time. Family volunteering strengthens the family, addresses critical social needs, and improves employee morale. Families are starving for quality time, and this is a good way to obtain it. In 1996, Carnival Cruise Lines formed Friends Uniting Neighbors for their employees to do volunteer work with their families. FUN plans biweekly activities, and more than 700 employees participate annually. Not only does family volunteering boost morale and develop leadership, but it also gives family members a better appreciation of what they have and shows the community the company cares. The Points of Light Foundation, a nonprofit organization in Washington, D.C., offers special training and technical assistance in family volunteering. Such companies as Target Corporation, Motorola, Inc., Sears Roebuck and Company, and the Allstate Corporation sponsor such family things as volunteering at shelters for abused animals, teaching literacy at low-income housing projects, working with terminally ill

As the only employees in the office who didn't have daughters selling Girl Scout cookies, Ron and Greg were hunted down like animals.

children, and distributing blankets and toys to a Skid Row mission. Many believe that family volunteering is the wave of the future!

 Several years ago the Professional Speakers of Illinois decided they wanted to sponsor a service project that included families. They

161

chose to support an organization called *"Cheerful Givers," which encourages groups to prepare children's birthday bags* to be distributed at food pantries and shelters. Robin Maynard, the founder of Cheerful Givers, discovered that parents on welfare often have no money to buy their child a birthday gift, so she decided to make birthday bags available for them to give to their children. For the Illinois project, Cheerful Givers supplied the tissue paper and decorated Happy Birthday bags. Then each family was asked to bring 25 of any one item to put into the bags. Depending on the family's budget, they brought items such as crayons and coloring books, reading books, candy and packs of gum, small stuffed animals, pens, matchbox cars, toothbrushes, and various other things a child would like. Then the contributions were spread out on tables in piles of ten. Each family took a birthday bag and lined it with colored tissue and then filled it with ten different items. The most special part of this project was that family members of any age could participate, from choosing what item to buy to actually putting the contents in the bag. In fact, our group included grandparents as well as toddlers. As a result of this family group effort, 120 children in Illinois received birthday bags that summer! The event ended with a potluck dinner. (For more information on Cheerful Givers, see Resources at the back of this book.)

 For the second straight year, Nationwide Insurance claims personnel and salespeople of the Knoxville office have participated in *"Ringing the Bell" for the Salvation Army.* They scheduled a full day for being responsible for the "Bell Station" at the Kmart near one of the claims offices. Beginning at 10 AM until 8 PM on one day in December, employees, their wives, and children took turns ringing the bell and wishing everyone a Merry Christmas. Caps were provided with the Nationwide brand to show their support of the community.

 NationsBank not only offers a $25 a week credit for childcare for employees who earn $30,000 a year or less, but they also allow employees two hours of *paid time off every week to spend with their children.* The company urges childless workers to take the time off too, and to spend it working with community-based youth programs.

 Prudential Insurance Company has started a PruKids Program that *recognizes the children of Prudential employees who performed outstanding, self-initiated acts of community service.* Prudential employees have volunteered 76,000 hours in communities where they live and work through company-sponsored events.

 Jan Simon, the vice president of human resources at Xerox Color Grafx in San Jose, California, shared that her company holds *family nights on Tuesday at the local food bank.* The families also paint and fix up homes for the elderly on the weekends.

> **The only ones among us who will be truly happy are those who have sought and found how to serve.**
>
> Albert Schweitzer

Do community-service projects with coworkers. This not only benefits the chosen charity, but it also promotes team building.

 A few years ago the employees of the city of Thomasville, Georgia, began preparing *Christmas stockings for the Salvation Army.* The project has gotten bigger and bigger each year, and many employees contribute up to five stockings for varying ages of children.

The University of Utah Hospitals and Clinics in Salt Lake City does many things to serve their community. Wendy Bailey, the Coordinator of Employee Services, shared several of their creative service programs:

 "Blue Jeans for Babies"—This was a community service project in which any employee could pay a small amount to wear blue jeans to work on a certain day. This money went to the *March of Dimes.*

 "Reading Marathon"—On November 5, 2002, the *employees donated books and money to buy books* to encourage kids in the community to read. Clifford, the literary mascot, came for the day and handed out fruit snacks to the patients and their visitors as well as visiting all the children in the hospital and encouraging them to read. The hospital donated new books for newborns and took pictures of them with their parents. Some of the employees read to children at the libraries and schools in the city that day, and the hospital gave books away to employees and their families. They also sponsored a reading marathon for 30 days. Children who read every night for the entire time were invited to a party in the convention center after the first of the year.

 "You Can Create Magic!"—Employees *donated children's games, books, gently used clothing, and educational materials to a local school with limited resources.* They placed containers at all the hospitals and clinics to create awareness that education is important. Many staff members also went to the school to read to the children to encourage them to continue their education.

 "Holiday Food Drive"—The goal for 2002 was 7,000 pounds of food as well as donations of dollars. When an employee donates one dollar, it buys $13 of food from local stores. In 2001 the University of Utah Hospitals and Clinics donated 5,000 pounds of food and more than $1,000.

 "Under the Big Top"—The organization invites the entire community for a *Health Fair,* especially anyone in the valley with children. They host a circus with mascots, cotton candy, and hot dogs, and they invite other community agencies such as the police, fire department, and emergency services. They provide information to families on such things as seat-belt safety, car-seat safety, and where to get health services such as free flu shots. It becomes a special outing for the whole family!

Encourage service to others. In my book *Handle with CARE—Motivating and Retaining Employees,* I wrote about ways different organizations are encouraging their employees to serve:

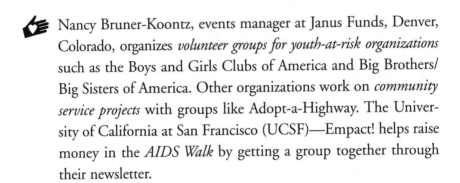

Nancy Bruner-Koontz, events manager at Janus Funds, Denver, Colorado, organizes *volunteer groups for youth-at-risk organizations* such as the Boys and Girls Clubs of America and Big Brothers/ Big Sisters of America. Other organizations work on *community service projects* with groups like Adopt-a-Highway. The University of California at San Francisco (UCSF)—Empact! helps raise money in the *AIDS Walk* by getting a group together through their newsletter.

At Tom's of Maine the policy is that *employees should try to donte 5 percent of their work time* to some kind of community service or volunteer project. This encourages employees to explore their gifts as they help others.

Ashland Chemical in Dublin, Ohio, *gives scientists company time to make presentations to science classes* and also dedicates space for a group of students to meet to conduct science research. They also donate used fitness equipment from their fitness centers to a United Way agency that sponsors fitness centers for inner-city families.

The Rockport Company organized a group of employees to *paint the storage facility for a local food pantry.*

BI Performance Services in Minneapolis, Minnesota, has *many volunteer groups.* Some of these groups help those in the community and others are internal volunteers. Here are a few of them:
- ***Bridging Team***—The team raises money as well as communicating, coordinating, and staffing *monthly household goods col-*

lections of items donated by BI associates. Their goal is to provide quality furniture and household goods for the economically disadvantaged.

- **Corporate Orientation Team**—This team has been volunteering for a number of years to *help new associates* learn about what's important at BI. They cover benefits, telephones, history and culture, and quality and customer satisfaction.

- **Loaves and Fishes Team**—Since 1992, the Loaves and Fishes Team has *served a meal once a month* to anyone who wishes to join them at Creekside in Bloomington. On an average night they serve 75 meals. They also collect donations from BI associates.

- **Recycling Committee**—Their mission is to *reduce waste* at BI through recycling and use reduction, education, and reward as their main tools. Through the year they reward associates with goodies such as caramel apples, cookies, state fair coupon booklets, calendars, etc. They visit individual departments, as needed, and do educational stints in addition to their cardboard crunching, can crushing, and dumpster diving all around BI!

- **Tour Guides**—They take time from their regular work schedule to *act as hosts* to clients to showcase the BI campus and explain how BI's departments work together. They know the ins and outs from Accounting to the Warehouse!

- **Singing Recognition Team**—This group *sings* throughout BI. You give them the words to use and they'll match them to a tune.

> The greatest use of life is to spend it for something that will outlast it.
>
> William James

They have sung to more than 150 associates in team meetings or at their desks.[2]

As an organization, build something for the community in which you are located

 Habitat for Humanity will organize building projects for organizations that want to help build low-income housing. They also sponsor weekend work trips that work teams can attend together. If you would like a team-building experience while at the same time helping your community, this is a wonderful resource. They do all the organizing; your organization does all the labor!

 In my hometown of Harlan, Iowa, a young man who worked at the local newspaper decided that the town needed a new playground, so he began to organize a community-wide project to first of all raise the funds and then to actually build a playground for the children of the community. The wonderful part of this project was that the entire town got involved. Companies donated food and water, building materials, and manpower. Retired people baked cookies and made sandwiches for the workers, the schoolchildren decorated grocery bags to sell at the local store to raise funds, and the *Harlan Tribune,* which sponsored the project, kept the community informed of the needs and the progress.

Sponsor collections. This is an easy way to help your employees blend work and service. You can collect food for a food drive or gently used clothing and household items for residents of public housing, Christmas gifts for needy children, or even school supplies to be delivered to schools with disadvantaged students. You can plan your drives to coincide with different holidays during the year or you can do them at odd times to make it less stressful and more fun.

Encourage service sabbaticals and personal growth leaves. Wells Fargo, UPS, and Xerox offer programs like these so their employees can have time to rewind and serve others.

 Compaq Computers, Inc., of Cupertino, California, offers its 8,500 employees a paid *six-week sabbatical every four years of continuous employment to make public-service commitments.* This might be extended to nine weeks with accrued vacation time. These sabbaticals have been spent on domestic and international projects ranging from working with underprivileged Appalachian children to training women in West Africa to raise cattle. They also provide travel and living expenses for employees who spend at least three weeks working with a nonprofit agency.

> The greatest use of life is to spend it for something that will outlast it.
>
> William James

8

Putting It All Together— The Importance of Anchors

Now THAT WE have explored all the areas of your life, ask yourself the question, "What have I done this week to blend:
- Work and Family?
- Work and Friends?
- Work and Health?
- Work and Spirit?
- Work and Service?"

Even if you have done only one thing in each of these areas, be proud of yourself. You have become aware of, conscious of, and deliberate about blending!

As I mentioned in the preface, it is ironic that as I write this book on balance and blending, I am at a point in my life in which my balance is more precarious than it has ever been! What I have discovered through all of this, however, is that our lights can continue to shine as beacons to guide others as long as we have **anchors** to hold on to. Just as the lighthouse stands firm to keep the ships from crashing upon the shore, the anchors we choose in life keep us focused and "on track." Although some of my anchors have changed drastically in the past two years, I have realized that others have become even more important in my life, and these include my faith, my family, my friends, and the National Speakers Association.

As you think about ways you can incorporate the ideas in this book to blend work and the other important parts of your life, it is vitally important to become aware of your anchors, especially the anchors that do not depend on your job:

- Who or what gives you a sense of belonging, of rootedness, of security?
- Who or what is important to keep you focused and conscious of heading in the right direction in your life?
- Who or what would leave a huge void in your life if they/it went away?
- Who or what do you value more than most other things in your life?
- Where do you find your identity as a unique individual?
- Who would miss you if you were gone?

LIST YOUR ANCHORS HERE:

If you realize that you don't have any anchors in your life outside of your job, make it a priority to find some. Join a support group, a hobby group, a professional organization, or a church or synagogue. Focus on one or two special friends and work on developing a close, sharing relationship with them. Are there family members you are particularly close to? If so, work on cultivating a new, closer relationship with them. Even if you do not fully realize it, you may have some anchors in your life, perhaps as simple as the relationships with the people you ride with on the train each day to work. These anchors will give you stability and balance as you work on a new way of approaching your life.

The latest in specialty parenting magazines.

Conclusion:
Taking Care of Ourselves

Let us take care of the children, for they have a long way to go. Let us take care of the elders, for they have come a long way. Let us take care of those in between, for they are doing the work.

Traditional African prayer

HAVE YOU NOTICED that sometimes when we write something or prepare new material, it is partly because we need the reminder ourselves? How true that is of this book! Just last week I was with a dear speaker friend who was showing me a wonderful new workbook he had created for an upcoming program. As I thumbed through it, a checklist about how motivational energy levels can be increased struck me. They included:
- Complete physical exam each year
- Balanced, reduced-fat, controlled-calorie diet
- At least 64 ounces of water every day

- Physician-directed dietary supplements (vitamins, fiber, etc.)
- Aerobic and strength training three times a week
- Sufficient amounts of sound sleep every night
- Mind-body health exercises (positive self-talk, meditation, etc.)
- Spiritual affirmation through your personal belief system
- Following the same schedule every day, including weekends
- Intelligent use of alcohol and tobacco

The real irony was that while he was prescribing these behaviors for his audiences, he was doing very few of them in his own life!

As committed employees and family members, we constantly give so much to our work and to our families that we often have little energy left for ourselves. My personal brand is "Regenerating Spirit—Creating Cultures Where People Matter," and I focus on Regenerating Spirit in the Workplace, in the Home, in your Customers, and in Yourself. I have found that in most organizations, in most homes, and even in most individuals, the primary focus is on the *external* rather than the *internal,* and I am no exception. What I keep learning and relearning, however, is that until our own spirits are renewed, it is very difficult to renew the spirits of others.

Stephen Covey first wrote about the concept of the "Emotional Bank Account," which says, basically, that during our day we get deposits and we get withdrawals. When we have withdrawal after withdrawal, we end up bankrupt, and in that state we can do little good for anyone. In my presentations I ask my audiences to think about how, when they realize their own emotional bank accounts are low, they can give themselves deposits. As employees and family members, we are constantly depositing into the emotional bank accounts of others, so it is critically important that we keep a close eye on our own balance.

I've had some really huge withdrawals in my emotional bank account over the years, including losing a child and the recent death of my husband. Because I am alone and because, just like all of you, I have a deep sense of mission about my work, I often find lately that I am working all the time, and that becomes another withdrawal. Sometimes working all the time is also an anesthetic to avoid the reality of the pain of our personal situations.

> **We may run, walk, stumble, drive, or fly, but let us never lose sight of the reason for the journey, or miss a chance to see a rainbow on the way.**
>
> Gloria Gaither

Most of the time, however, I consciously try to make the effort to refill my emotional bank account so that I will be able to give my full self to my audiences.

Here are some ways that I have found to do that:

 Keeping a Blessings Journal. At the end of each day I write the names of people who have made a difference in my life that day. It is amazing that even on the worst days, there are still blessings!

 Giving myself permission to have fun. Whether I am shopping, getting a manicure, going to a movie I've wanted to see, or simply walking on the beach, at least once a week I try to do something just for me. Daily, I do simple things like taking five-minute vacations or calling someone who loves me.

 Reading something that brings me joy. The way I balance this is that when I am on a business trip, I make a deal with myself—on the way there I catch up on business reading, but on the way back I get to read "fun" stuff.

 Planning to be with people I love or want to get to know. At least once a week I make definite plans to be with at least one good friend and at least one person I'd like to get to know better. During busy travel weeks I have to do this by phone or I schedule time with people in the cities where I am speaking. This helps me keep my problems in perspective.

 Appreciating others. I spend a few hours each week (sometimes longer) thanking people who have made a difference in my life. Even though this is a form of giving, it always refills my emotional bank account.

 Having some quiet time each day. This is my time for prayer, reflection, spiritual reading, and centering. I call these moments "Pockets of Peace," and they can be found anywhere—in the woods, in the car, in doctor's offices, and on airplanes.

 Exercising. When I am at my new home in Sarasota, Florida, I walk on the beach and/or swim a mile every day. When I am in Illinois, I spend 40 minutes on my treadmill. Often I walk with a friend and we talk as much (or more) than we walk!

Think about what you can do for yourself to keep your own emotional bank account full and write down at least two things. Then use that as an actionable strategy to take CARE of yourself. As I was writing this book, I was reminded that for the past three months I have been wanting to get a massage, and yet I let everything else get in the way of doing that. I am calling for an appointment first thing in the morning!

We have an awesome responsibility and a precious blessing in the work we do and in the families we have been blessed with. We must keep ourselves refilled and renewed so that we can truly be our best selves and make a difference in the lives of others. As you begin to incorporate some of the ideas in this book, your life will become a blended and unique work of art, and you will no longer have to feel guilty. And when you look back on your whole life many years from now, I hope you will see that you did achieve the balance for which you strived.

I want to close with a wonderful story about a man who decided to use marbles to help him focus on the really important things in life. He figured that the average person today lives about 75 years. Then he multiplied 75 times 52 and came up with 3,900, which is the number of Saturdays that the average person has in his or her entire lifetime. He decided to buy enough marbles to represent each of the Saturdays he had left in his "average" lifetime, which came to 1,000, and he put them in a large, clear-plastic container. Then every Saturday

> The most beautiful people we have known are those who have known defeat, known suffering, known struggle, known loss, and have found their way out of the depths. These persons have an appreciation, sensitivity, and an understanding of life that fills them with compassion, gentleness, and a deep loving concern. Beautiful people do not just happen.
>
> Elizabeth Kubler-Ross

he took one marble out of the jar and threw it away. As he watched the marbles diminish, he became more and more focused on what was really important. His lesson: There is nothing like watching your time here on this earth run out to help you get your priorities straight. How many marbles do you have left?

One of the great lies of organizational life is that jobs can be as big as the people who fill them. It's not true. Teams can never be as big as our families. Colleagues can never be as big as our friends. Companies can never be as rich, as wonderful, as the people in them. We are bigger than organizations. We just are.

William Gartner, USC Professor

May God fill our lives with important work, laughter, love, and tears of joy!

Barbara Glanz
December 13, 2002
Sarasota, Florida

INDIVIDUAL ACTIVITIES

How Do Children Feel about Working Parents? Use the following questions to begin a discussion with your child about your work. You might be surprised at some of the answers!

1. What kind of work does your (mom, dad) do? Who does your (mom, dad) work for? Where does (she, he) work?

2. What is your work?

3. Why do you think your (mom, dad) goes to work?

4. What do you do while your parent or parents work?

5. What would happen if your (mom, dad) didn't work?

6. What are the good things about your parent or parents working?

7. What are the bad things?

8. How does your (mom, dad) feel about (her, his) work?

9. How would you like things to be different?

ORGANIZATIONAL ACTIVITIES

How "Family-Friendly" Are You? Permission has been granted by Bonnie Michaels, President of Managing Work and Family, to share this survey. I have added some categories to the original survey published by Michaels. *Check the appropriate space.*

	Yes	No
Dependent Care Initiatives		
Childcare Resource and Referral	☐	☐
Eldercare Consultation and Referral	☐	☐
Respite Care Program	☐	☐
Sick/Emergency Childcare Program	☐	☐
On- or Near-Site Childcare Center	☐	☐
Consortium Childcare Center	☐	☐
Adult Day Care Center	☐	☐
Intergenerational Day Care	☐	☐
Summer/Holiday Care Program	☐	☐
Before- and After-School Programs	☐	☐
Caregiver Fairs	☐	☐
Employee Support Groups	☐	☐
Family Day at Work (or similar annual event)	☐	☐
Other Dependent Care Services	☐	☐

	Yes	*No*

Unpaid Leaves of Absence

	Yes	*No*
Maternity/Disability	☐	☐
Parental (maternal and/or paternal)	☐	☐
Adoption	☐	☐
Family	☐	☐
Personal	☐	☐
Sabbatical	☐	☐
Social Service Leave	☐	☐
Bereavement Leave	☐	☐
Sickness-in-Family Leave	☐	☐
Leave Sharing	☐	☐
Leave Bank	☐	☐
Nursing Breaks	☐	☐

Paid Leaves of Absence (Salary and/or Benefits, in full or in part)

	Yes	*No*
Maternity/Disability	☐	☐
Parental (maternal and/or paternal)	☐	☐
Adoption	☐	☐
Family	☐	☐
Personal	☐	☐
Sabbatical	☐	☐
Social Service Leave	☐	☐
Bereavement Leave	☐	☐
Sickness-in-Family Leave	☐	☐
Leave Sharing	☐	☐

	Yes	No
Leave Bank	☐	☐
Nursing Breaks	☐	☐

Financial Benefits

	Yes	No
Cafeteria Plan Benefits	☐	☐
Long-Term Health Care Insurance	☐	☐
Adoption Assistance	☐	☐
Corporate Discounts (i.e., with childcare providers, health clubs, etc.)	☐	☐
Reserved Slots in Childcare Centers	☐	☐
Vouchers	☐	☐
DCAP/Flexible Spending Accounts	☐	☐
Company Reimbursement of Dependent Care Caused by Business Travel or Overtime	☐	☐
Tuition Subsidies or Grants	☐	☐
College Scholarships for Children of Employees	☐	☐
Employee-Assisted Housing	☐	☐
Other Financial Assistance	☐	☐

Flexible Work Arrangements

	Yes	No
Flextime	☐	☐
Flexplace/Work at Home	☐	☐
Regular Part-time Work	☐	☐
Phase-In from Leave	☐	☐
Phase-Out Retirement	☐	☐
Job Sharing	☐	☐

	Yes	*No*
Telecommuting	☐	☐
Compressed Workweek	☐	☐
Pool of Temporary Workers	☐	☐
Vacation Time Sharing	☐	☐
Overtime Flexibility	☐	☐
"V-Time" (Voluntarily Reduced Time)— Individual Schedules	☐	☐
Family-Compatible Shift Schedules—Predictable and Flexible	☐	☐
Task Contracting	☐	☐
Other Flexible Work Arrangements	☐	☐

Education/Employee Services

Handbook of Work/Family Benefits and Policies	☐	☐
Designated Work and Family Program Manager	☐	☐
Ongoing Work and Family Committee or Task Force	☐	☐
Employee Assistance Program (EAP)	☐	☐
Wellness Program	☐	☐
Work/Family Seminars or Workshops	☐	☐
Support Groups	☐	☐
Childcare Handbook/Guidebook	☐	☐
Eldercare Handbook/Guidebook	☐	☐
Working Parents' Newsletter	☐	☐
Parent Resource Center	☐	☐
Stress Reduction Seminars	☐	☐
Time Management Seminars	☐	☐

	Yes	No
Hotlines	☐	☐
Resource Library	☐	☐
Relocation Assistance—Working Spouses	☐	☐
Relocation Assistance—Unmarried Partners	☐	☐
Relocation Assistance—Children/Families	☐	☐
Family Support Services after Workforce Reductions or Plant Closings	☐	☐

RESOURCES

Alliance for Work-Life Professionals
Conferences
515 King Street, Suite 420
Alexandria, VA 22314
800-874-9383
<www.awlp.org>

Boston College Center for
Work and Family
Research
140 Commonwealth Ave.
Chestnut Hill, MA 02467
617-552-2844
<www.bc.edu/centers/cwf>

Catalyst
Research
120 Wall Street, Floor 5
New York, NY 10005
212-514-7600

Cheerful Givers
28530 97th St. NW
Zimmerman, MN 55398
763-633-1604
<www.cheerfulgivers.org>
Contact: Robin Maynard
rmaynard@visi.com

Child Care Action Campaign
330 Seventh Ave., 14th Floor
New York, NY 10001
212-239-0138
<www.childcareaction.org>

Conference Board
Research and Reports
845 Third Ave.
New York, NY 10022
212-759-0900
<www.conference-board.org>

Families and Work Institute
Research and Reports
267 Fifth Ave., Floor 2
New York, NY 10016
212-465-2044
<www.familiesandwork.org>
Contact: Ellen Galinsky

Family Support of America
Community & Corporate Programs/Initiatives
20 N. Wacker Drive, Suite 1100
Chicago, IL 60606
312-338-0900
<www.familysupportamerica.org>

John McPherson, Cartoonist
Close to Home
<www.closetohome.com>

Work & Family Connection, Inc.
Online Research/Trend Reports
5197 Beachside Dr.
Minnetonka, MN 55343
800-487-7898
<www.workfamily.com>
Contact: Susan Seitel
susan@workfamily.com

IMPORTANT LINKS

Work-family or Work-life:

LifeCare

Employee Services Management Association
<www.esmassn.org>

College/University Work/Family Association
<www.cuwfa.org>

Work & Family Life Newsletter (e-mail)
workfam@aol.com

Parenting:

Parents Helping Parents
<www.php.com>

Parent Information Network
<http://npin.org>

Parent Soup
<www.parentsoup.com>

Family World
<www.family.com>

Parents Place
<www.parentsplace.com>

BlueSuitMom.com
<www.bluesuitmom.com>

Eldercare:

Joy Loverde (e-mail)
joyloverde@elderindustry.com

Elder Care On Line
<www.ec-online.net>

Other:

InnerWork Technologies, Inc.
<www.wisdomatwork.com>

Family Products:

Family Table Time

ENDNOTES

PREFACE

1. National Institute of Business Management, "Work, family pressures undercut job satisfaction," *Work/Life Today,* 2. (For more information on the study *Workplace Trends: America's Attitudes about Work, Employers, and Government,* contact Carl Van Horn or Herbert Schaffner, Heldrich Center for Workforce Development, Rutgers University, 732-932-4100.)

INTRODUCTION

1. Aon Consulting, *America@Work Study 1998.* 800-438-6487; www.aon.com.

2. Editor, "Time-Stressed Consumers?" *Entrepreneur,* December 1999, 120. A study by the Families and Work Institute (FWI).

3. Editor, "The 'family guy' lives: Young men will trade money for time," *Success in Recruiting & Retaining* newsletter, July 2000, 4. Study at the Radcliffe Public Policy Center, Cambridge, Mass.

4. National Institute of Business Management, *Work/Life Today,* 2. Study titled *Workplace Trends: America's Attitudes about Work, Employers, and Government.*

5. Joel Levey and Michelle Levey, *Living in Balance—A Dynamic Approach for Creating Harmony & Wholeness in a Chaotic World* (Berkeley, Calif.: Conari Press, 1998), 249–50.

6. Editor, "Why Are Americans Always in a Rush?" *USA Today,* 2 April 2001, sec. A, p. 1.

CHAPTER 1: A FOUNDATION

1. Joel Levey and Michelle Levey, *Living in Balance—A Dynamic Approach for Creating Harmony & Wholeness in a Chaotic World* (Berkeley, Calif.: Conari Press, 1998), 48–49.

2. Ibid., 49.

3. Barbara A. Glanz, *Handle with CARE—Motivating & Retaining Employees* (New York: McGraw-Hill, 2002), 29.

CHAPTER 2: UNDERSTANDING AND CLARIFYING THE DIFFERENT FACETS OF OUR LIVES

1. H. Stanley Jones, *Quality of Life—Achieving Balance in an Unbalanced World* (Kauai, Hawaii: Kauai Press, 1994), 149.

CHAPTER 3: BLENDING WORK AND FAMILY

1. Kathy Bergen and Stephen Franklin, "Getting respect for a life beyond work," *Chicago Tribune,* 4 June 1997, sec. 3, p. 4.

2. Editor, "How Much Is Enough," *Fast Company* 26, July/August 1999, 108–16.

3. Nicola Godfrey, "Sarah Lightens Up," *Working Woman,* October 1999, 30.

4. Barbara A. Glanz, *CARE Packages for the Home—Dozens of Ways to Regenerate Spirit Where You Live* (Kansas City, Mo.: Andrews-McMeel, 1998), 21.

5. Nancy Evans, "The New Consciousness Raising," *Working Woman,* October 1999, 24.

6. Hewitt Associates, *Work/Life Benefits Provided by Major U.S. Employers in 2001–2002,* Lincolnshire, Ill.; 847-295-5000; www .hewitt.com.

7. National Institute of Business Management, "Prudential's Life-Works program yields $6 million in savings," *Work/Life Today,* 6.

8. Employee Services Management Association, "Family Activities Conveniently Create Quality Time," *ESM Magazine,* March 1995, 9.

9. Employee Services Management Association, *ESM Magazine,* 1995. Reprinted with permission.

10. Jennifer J. Laabs, "Kids Become Employees for a Day," *Personnel Journal,* July 1993, 64.

11. Employee Services Management Association, "Family Activities Conveniently Create Quality Time," 9.

12. Ibid.

13. Ibid.

14. Ibid.

15. Bonnie Miller Rubin, "Kindness on job comfort families at home," *Chicago Tribune,* 28 October 2001, 1–2.

16. Barbara A. Glanz, *Handle with CARE—Motivating & Retaining Employees* (New York: McGraw-Hill, 2002), 241–42.

17. Carol Leonetti Dannhauser, "The Right Rewards," *Working Woman,* July/August 2000, 40–41.

18. Editor, "Quick Tip," *Success in Recruiting and Retaining,* December 2000.

19. Carol Kleiman, "Family-friendly benefits snub singles, they say," *Chicago Tribune,* 18 December 2001, sec. 3, p. 1.

20. Andrea C. Poe, "The Baby Blues," *HR Magazine,* July 2000, 79.

21. Charles Fishman, "Moving Toward a Balanced Work Life," *Workforce Magazine,* March 2000, 38–42.

22. Baird K. Brightman, "Letter to the Editor," *Fast Company,* June/July 1998, 32.

CHAPTER 4: BLENDING WORK AND FRIENDS

1. Joel Levey and Michelle Levey, *Living in Balance—A Dynamic Approach for Creating Harmony & Wholeness in a Chaotic World* (Berkeley, Calif.: Conari Press, 1998), 186–87.

2. Barbara Moses, Ph.D., "Are We Working Ourselves to Death?" *Training,* November 1998, 40.

3. Barbara Moses, Ph.D., "The Busyness Trap," *Training,* November 1998, 39.

4. Krista Kurth, Ph.D., and Suzanne Adele Schmidt, Ph.D., *Running on Plenty at Work: Renewal Strategies for Individuals* (Potomac, Md.: Renewal Resources Press, 2003).

5. Catrina Cerny, "The Young and the Restless: Serving the New Generation of Employees," *Employee Services Management* magazine, September 1998, 14.

6. Society for Human Resource Management, "Important Steps for Implementing Diversity Training," *Mosaics,* July/August 2002, 5.

CHAPTER 5: BLENDING WORK AND HEALTH

1. Mary Beth Sammons, "Walkers find an inside track to spirituality," *Chicago Tribune,* 13 October 1999, sec. 8, p. 6.

2. Krista Kurth, Ph.D., and Suzanne Adele Schmidt, Ph.D., *Running on Plenty at Work: Renewal Strategies for Individuals* (Potomac, Md.: Renewal Resources Press, 2003).

3. Nicola Godfrey, "Sarah Lightens Up," *Working Woman,* October 1999, 30.

4. Editor, "In Search of the Work/Life Balance," *ExecutiveFEMALE,* August 2000, 2.

5. National Institute of Business Management, "Lactation programs get new moms back on the job," *Work/Life Today,* 4.

6. Barbara A. Glanz, *CARE Packages for the Workplace—Dozens of Little Things You Can Do to Regenerate Spirit at Work* (New York: McGraw-Hill, 1996), 171.

7. Bonnie Michaels, "Helping Families Reduce Work-Life Stress," *America's Family Support Magazine,* Summer 2001, 38.

8. National Institute of Business Management, "Lactation programs get new moms back on the job."

9. Editor, "Worth Noting," *BusinessEthics,* January/February 2000, 7.

10. Editor, "What's New," *HR Magazine,* September 2002, 142.

CHAPTER 6: BLENDING WORK AND SPIRIT

1. Joel Levey and Michelle Levey, *Living in Balance—A Dynamic Approach for Creating Harmony & Wholeness in a Chaotic World* (Berkeley, Calif.: Conari Press, 1998), 187–88.

2. Ibid., 186–87.

3. Roger E. Herman and Joyce L. Gioia, *Lean and Meaningful: A New Culture for Corporate America* (Winchester, Va.: Oakhill Press, 1998), 6–7.

4. Frederic M. Hudson, *Mastering the Art of Self-Renewal: Adulthood as Continual Revitalization* (New York: MJF Books, 2002), in Krista Kurth, Ph.D., and Suzanne Adele Schmidt, Ph.D., *Running on Plenty at Work: Renewal Strategies for Individuals* (Potomac, Md.: Renewal Resources Press, 2003).

5. David Dorsey, "The New Spirit of Work," *Fast Company,* August 1998, 130.

6. Diane E. Lewis, "Spiritual revival revealed in workplace—Some workers seek more than just a job," *Boston Globe,* 16 December 2001.

7. Sarah Ban Breathnach, *The Simple Abundance Companion* (New York: Warner Books, 2000), in *Family Circle,* May 2000, 39.

8. Ann McGee-Cooper, with Duane Trammell, *You Don't Have to Go Home from Work Exhausted* (New York: Bantam Books, 1992).

9. Barbara A. Glanz, *Handle with CARE—Motivating & Retaining Employees* (New York: McGraw-Hill, 2002), 125–27.

10. Joel Levey and Michelle Levey, *Living in Balance,* 55.

11. Editor, "But when do they work?" *Work & Family Newsbrief,* Second Quarter 2002.

12. Editor, "This Is Not Your Father's Bargaining Agreement," *HR Magazine,* March 2001, 31.

13. Peter Carbonara, "Marriott Makes Room for Daddies," *Fast Company,* June/July 1998, 62–64.

14. Al Gini, "Religion in the Workplace," *The Works,* Summer 2000, 21.

15. Christopher Elliott, "Back to Basics," *Entrepreneur,* September 1999, 58.

16. Daniel Machalaba, "More Employees Are Seeking to Worship God on the Job," *Wall Street Journal,* 25 June 2002, sec. B, p. 1.

17. Ibid., p. 49.

18. Mary J. Nestor, "Top 7 Tips to Put Some 'Life' into Your Work," *Sharing Ideas* 23, no. 1 (October/November 2000): 20.

19. Bonnie Rubin Miller, *Time Out: How to Take a Year (or More or Less) Off Without Jeopardizing Your Job, Your Family, or Your Bank Account* (New York: W.W. Norton & Co., 1987).

20. Andrea C. Poe, "The Baby Blues," *HR Magazine,* July 2000, 82.

CHAPTER 7: BLENDING WORK AND SERVICE

1. Cedric B. Johnson, Ph.D., "When Working Harder is Not Smarter," *The Inner Edge,* April/May 2000, 18–21.

2. Barbara A. Glanz, *Handle with CARE—Motivating & Retaining Employees* (New York: McGraw-Hill, 2002), 233–35.

BIBLIOGRAPHY

Biggs, Dick. *If Life Is a Balancing Act, Why Am I So Darn Clumsy?* Roswell, Ga.: Chattahoochee Publishers, 1993.

Bravo, Ellen. *The Job/Family Challenge: Not for Women Only.* New York: John Wiley and Sons, 1995.

Covey, Stephen. *The Seven Habits of Highly Successful People.* New York: Fireside/Simon and Schuster, 1989.

Crosby, Faye J. *Juggling: The Unexpected Advantages of Balancing Career and Home for Women and Their Families.* New York: Free Press, 1993.

Editors. *Harvard Business Review on Work and Life Balance.* Boston: Harvard Business School Press, 2000.

Frogatt, Cynthia C. *Work Naked—Eight Essential Principles for Peak Performance in the Virtual Workplace.* San Francisco: Jossey-Bass, 2001.

Galinsky, Ellen; Stacy S. Kim; and James Bond. *Feeling Overworked: When Work Becomes Too Much.* New York: Families and Work Institute, 2001.

Greissman, Gene. *Time Tactics of Very Successful People.* New York: McGraw-Hill, 1994.

Herman, Roger E., and Joyce L. Gioia. *Lean and Meaningful: A New Culture for Corporate America.* Greensboro, N.C.: Oak Hill Press, 1998.

Jones, H. Stanley. *Quality of Life—Achieving Balance in an Unbalanced World.* Kauai, Hawaii: Kauai Press, 1994.

Kurth, Ph.D., Krista, and Suzanne Adele Schmidt, Ph.D. *Running on Plenty at Work: Renewal Strategies for Individuals.* Potomac, Md.: Renewal Resources Press, 2003.

Levey, Joel, and Michelle Levey. *Living in Balance—A Dynamic Approach for Creating Harmony & Wholeness in a Chaotic World.* Berkeley, Calif.: Conari Press, 1998.

Mackoff, Barbara. *The Art of Self-Renewal: Balancing Pressure and Productivity On and Off the Job.* Lowell House, 1993.

McDargh, Eileen. *Burnout, Balance, and Bounty.* Four Audio Cassette Series.

McDargh, Eileen. *Work for a Living and Still Be Free to Live.* Wilsonville, Ore.: BookPartners, Inc., 1999.

McDonald, Kathy, and Beth Sirull. *Creating Your Life Collage: Strategies for Solving the Work/Life Dilemma.* New York: Three Rivers Press, 2000.

McGee-Cooper, Ann. *You Don't Have to Go Home from Work Exhausted!* New York: Bantam Books, 1992.

Michaels, Bonnie, and Elizabeth C. McCarty. *Solving the Work/Family Puzzle.* Homewood, Ill.: Business One Irwin, 1992.

Nicholaus, Bret, and Paul Lowrie. *The Checkbook—200 Ways to Balance Your Life.* Novato, Calif.: New World Library, 1999.

Rogak, Lisa. *Smart Guide™ to Managing Your Time.* New York: Cedar Books, John Wiley and Sons, 1999.

Rogak, Lisa Angowski. *Time Off from Work—Using Sabbaticals to Enhance Your Life While Keeping Your Career on Track.* New York: John Wiley and Sons, 1994.

Rowinsky, Karen. "Take Care of Yourself While Caring for a Loved One—50 Easy Ways to Replenish Your Spirit, Refresh Your Attitude, and Recharge Your Life." <www.ComeAlivePresentations.com>, 2002. 866-269-3511.

Swiss, Deborah, and J. Walker. *Women and the Work/Family Dilemma: How Today's Professional Women Are Finding Solutions.* New York: John Wiley and Sons, 1993.

INDEX

ABOUT THE AUTHOR

BARBARA GLANZ, CSP, is a professional speaker, consultant, and author who specializes in "Regenerating Spirit—Creating Cultures Where People CARE™." She is an expert in motivation and retention, customer service, rewards and recognition, and blending work and home. Barbara works with organizations that want to improve morale, retention, and service and with people who want to rediscover the joy in their work and in their lives. She has written six books, has spoken on five continents and in 49 states, and lives and breathes her personal motto—"Spreading Contagious Enthusiasm™"—each day.

Barbara recently moved to Sarasota, Florida, from her longtime home in Western Springs, Illinois. She is the mother of three children on earth and one in heaven and the grandmother of Gavin William and Kinsey Clark Glanz. Her husband of 34 years, Charlie, died of lung cancer two years ago. She is deeply grateful to her friends and family for helping her make the transition to a new way of life, and her experience reinforces the idea that every day with our loved ones is a special gift to be cherished.

You can find out more information about Barbara and her work at <www.barbaraglanz.com>. If you have ideas of how you have blended work and home, please send them to her at bglanz@barbaraglanz.com.

Her other books include:

- *Handle with CARE—Motivating and Retaining Employees* (McGraw-Hill, 2002)

- *CARE Packages for the Workplace—Dozens of Little Things You Can Do to Regenerate Spirit at Work* (McGraw-Hill, 1996)
- *CARE Packages for the Home—Dozens of Ways to Regenerate Spirit Where You Live* (Andrews McMeel, 1998)
- *Building Customer Loyalty—How YOU Can Help Keep Customers Returning* (McGraw-Hill, 1994)
- *The Creative Communicator—399 Ways to Communicate Commitment without Boring People to Death!* (McGraw-Hill, 1998)

Share the message!

Bulk discounts
Discounts start at only 10 copies. Save up to 55% off retail price.

Custom publishing
Private label a cover with your organization's name and logo.
Or, tailor information to your needs with a custom pamphlet
that highlights specific chapters.

Ancillaries
Workshop outlines, videos, and other products are available on
select titles.

Dynamic speakers
Engaging authors are available to share their expertise and
insight at your event.